"After utilizing toolkits from The Art of Service, I was able to identify threats within my organization to which I was completely unaware. Using my team's knowledge as a competitive advantage, we now have superior systems that save time and energy."

"As a new Chief Technology Officer, I was feeling unprepared and inadequate to be successful in my role. I ordered an IT toolkit Sunday night and was prepared Monday morning to shed light on areas of improvement within my organization. I no longer felt overwhelmed and intimidated, I was excited to share what I had learned."

"I used the questionnaires to interview members of my team. I never knew how many insights we could produce collectively with our internal knowledge."

"I usually work until at least 8pm on weeknights. The Art of Service questionnaire saved me so much time and worry that Thursday night I attended my son's soccer game without sacrificing my professional obligations."

"After purchasing The Art of Service toolkit, I was able to identify areas where my company was not in compliance that could have put my job at risk. I looked like a hero when I proactively educated my team on the risks and presented a solid solution."

"I spent months shopping for an external consultant before realizing that The Art of Service would allow my team to consult themselves! Not only did we save time not catching a consultant up to speed, we were able to keep our company information and industry secrets confidential."

"Everyday there are new regulations and processes in my industry. The Art of Service toolkit has kept me ahead by using AI technology to constantly update the toolkits and address emerging needs."

"I customized The Art of Service toolkit to focus specifically on the concerns of my role and industry. I didn't have to waste time with a generic self-help book that wasn't tailored to my exact situation."

"Many of our competitors have asked us about our secret sauce. When I tell them it's the knowledge we have in-house, they never believe me. Little do they know The Art of Service toolkits are working behind the scenes."

"One of my friends hired a consultant who used the knowledge gained working with his company to advise their competitor. Talk about a competitive disadvantage! The Art of Service allowed us to keep our knowledge from walking out the door along with a huge portion of our budget in consulting fees."

"Honestly, I didn't know what I didn't know. Before purchasing The Art of Service, I didn't realize how many areas of my business needed to be refreshed and improved. I am so relieved The Art of Service was there to highlight our blind spots."

"Before The Art of Service, I waited eagerly for consulting company reports to come out each month. These reports kept us up to speed but provided little value because they put our competitors on the same playing field. With The Art of Service, we have uncovered unique insights to drive our business forward."

"Instead of investing extensive resources into an external consultant, we can spend more of our budget towards pursuing our company goals and objectives…while also spending a little more on corporate holiday parties."

"The risk of our competitors getting ahead has been mitigated because The Art of Service has provided us with a 360-degree view of threats within our organization before they even arise."

Applied behavior analysis
Complete Self-Assessment Guide

Notice of rights

You are licensed to use the Self-Assessment contents in your presentations and materials for internal use and customers without asking us - we are here to help.

All rights reserved for the book itself: this book may not be reproduced or transmitted in any form by any means, electronic, mechanical, photocopying, recording, or otherwise, without the prior written permission of the publisher.

The information in this book is distributed on an "As Is" basis without warranty. While every precaution has been taken in the preparation of the book, neither the author nor the publisher shall have any liability to any person or entity with respect to any loss or damage caused or alleged to be caused directly or indirectly by the instructions contained in this book or by the products described in it.

Trademarks

Many of the designations used by manufacturers and sellers to distinguish their products are claimed as trademarks. Where those designations appear in this book, and the publisher was aware of a trademark claim, the designations appear as requested by the owner of the trademark. All other product names and services identified throughout this book are used in editorial fashion only and for the benefit of such companies with no intention of infringement of the trademark. No such use, or the use of any trade name, is intended to convey endorsement or other affiliation with this book.

Copyright © by The Art of Service
https://theartofservice.com
support@theartofservice.com

Table of Contents

About The Art of Service — 10

Included Resources - how to access — 10
Purpose of this Self-Assessment — 12
How to use the Self-Assessment — 13
Applied behavior analysis
Scorecard Example — 15
Applied behavior analysis
Scorecard — 16

BEGINNING OF THE
SELF-ASSESSMENT: — 17
CRITERION #1: RECOGNIZE — 18

CRITERION #2: DEFINE: — 30

CRITERION #3: MEASURE: — 46

CRITERION #4: ANALYZE: — 61

CRITERION #5: IMPROVE: — 77

CRITERION #6: CONTROL: — 93

CRITERION #7: SUSTAIN: — 105
Applied behavior analysis and Managing Projects, Criteria for Project Managers: — 130
1.0 Initiating Process Group: Applied behavior analysis — 131

1.1 Project Charter: Applied behavior analysis — 133

1.2 Stakeholder Register: Applied behavior analysis — 135

1.3 Stakeholder Analysis Matrix: Applied behavior analysis — 136

2.0 Planning Process Group: Applied behavior analysis — 138

2.1 Project Management Plan: Applied behavior analysis 140

2.2 Scope Management Plan: Applied behavior analysis 142

2.3 Requirements Management Plan: Applied behavior analysis 144

2.4 Requirements Documentation: Applied behavior analysis 146

2.5 Requirements Traceability Matrix: Applied behavior analysis 148

2.6 Project Scope Statement: Applied behavior analysis 150

2.7 Assumption and Constraint Log: Applied behavior analysis 152

2.8 Work Breakdown Structure: Applied behavior analysis 154

2.9 WBS Dictionary: Applied behavior analysis 156

2.10 Schedule Management Plan: Applied behavior analysis 159

2.11 Activity List: Applied behavior analysis 161

2.12 Activity Attributes: Applied behavior analysis 163

2.13 Milestone List: Applied behavior analysis 165

2.14 Network Diagram: Applied behavior analysis 167

2.15 Activity Resource Requirements: Applied behavior analysis 169

2.16 Resource Breakdown Structure: Applied behavior analysis 171

2.17 Activity Duration Estimates: Applied behavior analysis 173

2.18 Duration Estimating Worksheet: Applied behavior analysis 175

2.19 Project Schedule: Applied behavior analysis 177

2.20 Cost Management Plan: Applied behavior analysis 179

2.21 Activity Cost Estimates: Applied behavior analysis 181

2.22 Cost Estimating Worksheet: Applied behavior analysis 183

2.23 Cost Baseline: Applied behavior analysis 185

2.24 Quality Management Plan: Applied behavior analysis 187

2.25 Quality Metrics: Applied behavior analysis 189

2.26 Process Improvement Plan: Applied behavior analysis 191

2.27 Responsibility Assignment Matrix: Applied behavior analysis 193

2.28 Roles and Responsibilities: Applied behavior analysis 195

2.29 Human Resource Management Plan: Applied behavior analysis 197

2.30 Communications Management Plan: Applied behavior analysis 199

2.31 Risk Management Plan: Applied behavior analysis 201

2.32 Risk Register: Applied behavior analysis 203

2.33 Probability and Impact Assessment: Applied behavior analysis 205

2.34 Probability and Impact Matrix: Applied behavior analysis 207

2.35 Risk Data Sheet: Applied behavior analysis 209

2.36 Procurement Management Plan: Applied behavior analysis 211

2.37 Source Selection Criteria: Applied behavior analysis 213

2.38 Stakeholder Management Plan: Applied behavior analysis 215

2.39 Change Management Plan: Applied behavior analysis 217

3.0 Executing Process Group: Applied behavior analysis 219

3.1 Team Member Status Report: Applied behavior analysis 221

3.2 Change Request: Applied behavior analysis 223

3.3 Change Log: Applied behavior analysis 225

3.4 Decision Log: Applied behavior analysis 227

3.5 Quality Audit: Applied behavior analysis 229

3.6 Team Directory: Applied behavior analysis 232

3.7 Team Operating Agreement: Applied behavior analysis 234

3.8 Team Performance Assessment: Applied behavior analysis 236

3.9 Team Member Performance Assessment: Applied behavior analysis 238

3.10 Issue Log: Applied behavior analysis 240

4.0 Monitoring and Controlling Process Group: Applied behavior analysis 242

4.1 Project Performance Report: Applied behavior analysis 244

4.2 Variance Analysis: Applied behavior analysis 246

4.3 Earned Value Status: Applied behavior analysis 248

4.4 Risk Audit: Applied behavior analysis 250

4.5 Contractor Status Report: Applied behavior analysis 252

4.6 Formal Acceptance: Applied behavior analysis 254

5.0 Closing Process Group: Applied behavior analysis 256

5.1 Procurement Audit: Applied behavior analysis 258

5.2 Contract Close-Out: Applied behavior analysis 260

5.3 Project or Phase Close-Out: Applied behavior analysis 262

5.4 Lessons Learned: Applied behavior analysis   264
Index   266

About The Art of Service

The Art of Service, Business Process Architects since 2000, is dedicated to helping stakeholders achieve excellence.

Defining, designing, creating, and implementing a process to solve a stakeholders challenge or meet an objective is the most valuable role… In EVERY group, company, organization and department.

Unless you're talking a one-time, single-use project, there should be a process. Whether that process is managed and implemented by humans, AI, or a combination of the two, it needs to be designed by someone with a complex enough perspective to ask the right questions.

Someone capable of asking the right questions and step back and say, 'What are we really trying to accomplish here? And is there a different way to look at it?'

With The Art of Service's Self-Assessments, we empower people who can do just that — whether their title is marketer, entrepreneur, manager, salesperson, consultant, Business Process Manager, executive assistant, IT Manager, CIO etc... —they are the people who rule the future. They are people who watch the process as it happens, and ask the right questions to make the process work better.

Contact us when you need any support with this Self-Assessment and any help with templates, blue-prints and examples of standard documents you might need:

https://theartofservice.com
support@theartofservice.com

Included Resources - how to access

Included with your purchase of the book is the Applied

behavior analysis Self-Assessment Spreadsheet Dashboard which contains all questions and Self-Assessment areas and auto-generates insights, graphs, and project RACI planning - all with examples to get you started right away.

How? Simply send an email to
access@theartofservice.com
with this books' title in the subject to get the Applied behavior analysis Self Assessment Tool right away.

The auto reply will guide you further, you will then receive the following contents with New and Updated specific criteria:

- The latest quick edition of the book in PDF

- The latest complete edition of the book in PDF, which criteria correspond to the criteria in...

- The Self-Assessment Excel Dashboard, and...

- Example pre-filled Self-Assessment Excel Dashboard to get familiar with results generation

- In-depth specific Checklists covering the topic

- Project management checklists and templates to assist with implementation

INCLUDES LIFETIME SELF ASSESSMENT UPDATES

Every self assessment comes with Lifetime Updates and Lifetime Free Updated Books. Lifetime Updates is an industry-first feature which allows you to receive verified self assessment updates, ensuring you always have the most accurate information at your fingertips.

Get it now- you will be glad you did - do it now, before you forget.

Send an email to **access@theartofservice.com** with this books' title in the subject to get the Applied behavior analysis Self Assessment Tool right away.

Purpose of this Self-Assessment

This Self-Assessment has been developed to improve understanding of the requirements and elements of Applied behavior analysis, based on best practices and standards in business process architecture, design and quality management.

It is designed to allow for a rapid Self-Assessment to determine how closely existing management practices and procedures correspond to the elements of the Self-Assessment.

The criteria of requirements and elements of Applied behavior analysis have been rephrased in the format of a Self-Assessment questionnaire, with a seven-criterion scoring system, as explained in this document.

In this format, even with limited background knowledge of Applied behavior analysis, a manager can quickly review existing operations to determine how they measure up to the standards. This in turn can serve as the starting point of a 'gap analysis' to identify management tools or system elements that might usefully be implemented in the organization to help improve overall performance.

How to use the Self-Assessment

On the following pages are a series of questions to identify to what extent your Applied behavior analysis initiative is complete in comparison to the requirements set in standards.

To facilitate answering the questions, there is a space in front of each question to enter a score on a scale of '1' to '5'.

1 Strongly Disagree

2 Disagree

3 Neutral

4 Agree

5 Strongly Agree

Read the question and rate it with the following in front of mind:

**'In my belief,
the answer to this question is clearly defined'.**

There are two ways in which you can choose to interpret this statement;
1. how aware are you that the answer to the question is clearly defined
2. for more in-depth analysis you can choose to gather evidence and confirm the answer to the question. This obviously will take more time, most Self-Assessment users opt for the first way to interpret the question and dig deeper later on based on the outcome of the overall Self-Assessment.

A score of '1' would mean that the answer is not clear at all, where a '5' would mean the answer is crystal clear and defined. Leave emtpy when the question is not applicable or you don't want to answer it, you can skip it without affecting your score. Write your score in the space provided.

After you have responded to all the appropriate statements in each section, compute your average score for that section, using the formula provided, and round to the nearest tenth. Then transfer to the corresponding spoke in the Applied behavior analysis Scorecard on the second next page of the Self-Assessment.

Your completed Applied behavior analysis Scorecard will give you a clear presentation of which Applied behavior analysis areas need attention.

Applied behavior analysis Scorecard Example

Example of how the finalized Scorecard can look like:

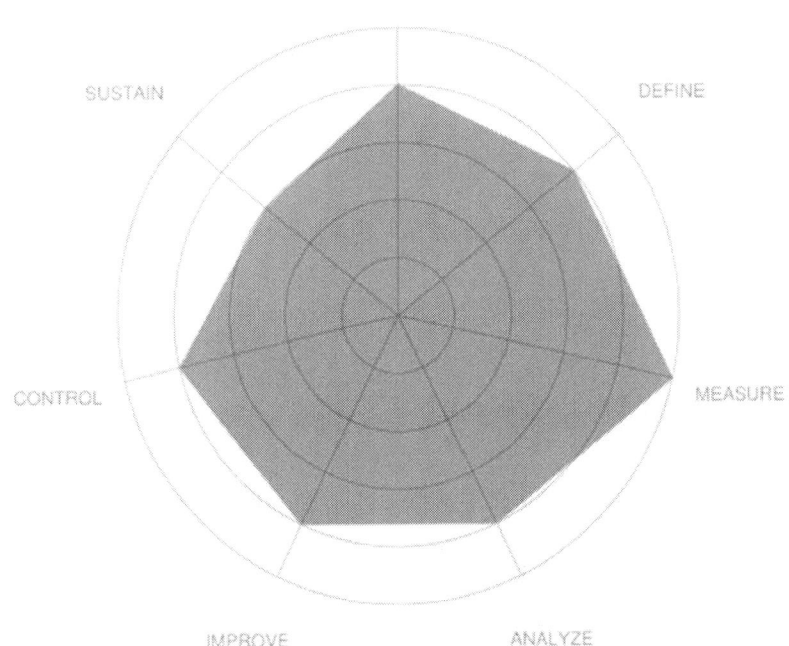

Applied behavior analysis Scorecard

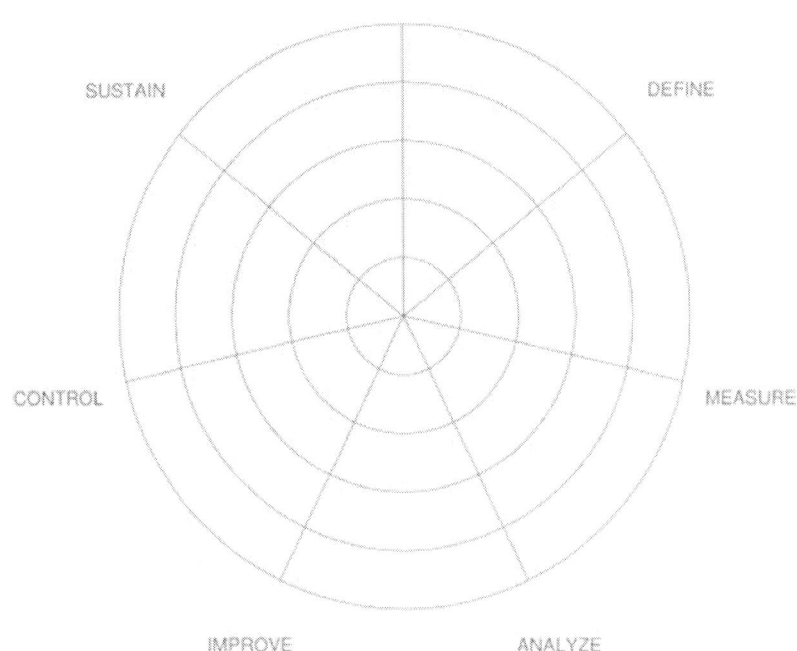

BEGINNING OF THE SELF-ASSESSMENT:

CRITERION #1: RECOGNIZE

INTENT: Be aware of the need for change. Recognize that there is an unfavorable variation, problem or symptom.

In my belief, the answer to this question is clearly defined:

5 Strongly Agree

4 Agree

3 Neutral

2 Disagree

1 Strongly Disagree

1. What training and capacity building actions are needed to implement proposed reforms?
<--- Score

2. What tools and technologies are needed for a custom Applied behavior analysis project?
<--- Score

3. What problems are you facing and how do you

consider Applied behavior analysis will circumvent those obstacles?
<--- Score

4. Do you need different information or graphics?
<--- Score

5. Will Applied behavior analysis deliverables need to be tested and, if so, by whom?
<--- Score

6. What prevents you from making the changes you know will make you a more effective Applied behavior analysis leader?
<--- Score

7. Who defines the rules in relation to any given issue?
<--- Score

8. How do you take a forward-looking perspective in identifying Applied behavior analysis research related to market response and models?
<--- Score

9. What needs to stay?
<--- Score

10. How do you identify subcontractor relationships?
<--- Score

11. Who needs budgets?
<--- Score

12. What are the expected benefits of Applied behavior analysis to the stakeholder?
<--- Score

13. How are you going to measure success?
<--- Score

14. To what extent would your organization benefit from being recognized as a award recipient?
<--- Score

15. Will new equipment/products be required to facilitate Applied behavior analysis delivery, for example is new software needed?
<--- Score

16. How do you identify the kinds of information that you will need?
<--- Score

17. Are there regulatory / compliance issues?
<--- Score

18. What are the timeframes required to resolve each of the issues/problems?
<--- Score

19. Looking at each person individually – does every one have the qualities which are needed to work in this group?
<--- Score

20. Which information does the Applied behavior analysis business case need to include?
<--- Score

21. What is the problem and/or vulnerability?
<--- Score

22. How do you recognize an objection?
<--- Score

23. To what extent does each concerned units management team recognize Applied behavior analysis as an effective investment?
<--- Score

24. Does Applied behavior analysis create potential expectations in other areas that need to be recognized and considered?
<--- Score

25. How do you recognize an Applied behavior analysis objection?
<--- Score

26. What does Applied behavior analysis success mean to the stakeholders?
<--- Score

27. Do you have/need 24-hour access to key personnel?
<--- Score

28. For your Applied behavior analysis project, identify and describe the business environment, is there more than one layer to the business environment?
<--- Score

29. Are employees recognized or rewarded for performance that demonstrates the highest levels of integrity?
<--- Score

30. What extra resources will you need?

<--- Score

31. What is the problem or issue?
<--- Score

32. What is the extent or complexity of the Applied behavior analysis problem?
<--- Score

33. How does it fit into your organizational needs and tasks?
<--- Score

34. Which needs are not included or involved?
<--- Score

35. Can management personnel recognize the monetary benefit of Applied behavior analysis?
<--- Score

36. What are the Applied behavior analysis resources needed?
<--- Score

37. Who needs what information?
<--- Score

38. How can auditing be a preventative security measure?
<--- Score

39. How many trainings, in total, are needed?
<--- Score

40. What would happen if Applied behavior analysis weren't done?

<--- Score

41. Are there Applied behavior analysis problems defined?
<--- Score

42. What do you need to start doing?
<--- Score

43. Are there any specific expectations or concerns about the Applied behavior analysis team, Applied behavior analysis itself?
<--- Score

44. Do you know what you need to know about Applied behavior analysis?
<--- Score

45. Would you recognize a threat from the inside?
<--- Score

46. Will a response program recognize when a crisis occurs and provide some level of response?
<--- Score

47. What information do users need?
<--- Score

48. What are your needs in relation to Applied behavior analysis skills, labor, equipment, and markets?
<--- Score

49. When a Applied behavior analysis manager recognizes a problem, what options are available?
<--- Score

50. What Applied behavior analysis problem should be solved?
<--- Score

51. Are problem definition and motivation clearly presented?
<--- Score

52. Who needs to know about Applied behavior analysis?
<--- Score

53. What is the Applied behavior analysis problem definition? What do you need to resolve?
<--- Score

54. Is the need for organizational change recognized?
<--- Score

55. What do employees need in the short term?
<--- Score

56. What vendors make products that address the Applied behavior analysis needs?
<--- Score

57. Are losses recognized in a timely manner?
<--- Score

58. Who else hopes to benefit from it?
<--- Score

59. Are you dealing with any of the same issues today as yesterday? What can you do about this?
<--- Score

60. Are there any revenue recognition issues?
<--- Score

61. Why the need?
<--- Score

62. Do you recognize Applied behavior analysis achievements?
<--- Score

63. What should be considered when identifying available resources, constraints, and deadlines?
<--- Score

64. Whom do you really need or want to serve?
<--- Score

65. Do you need to avoid or amend any Applied behavior analysis activities?
<--- Score

66. What creative shifts do you need to take?
<--- Score

67. What are the stakeholder objectives to be achieved with Applied behavior analysis?
<--- Score

68. Why is this needed?
<--- Score

69. How are training requirements identified?
<--- Score

70. Will it solve real problems?

<--- Score

71. Does your organization need more Applied behavior analysis education?
<--- Score

72. Is it needed?
<--- Score

73. As a sponsor, customer or management, how important is it to meet goals, objectives?
<--- Score

74. What Applied behavior analysis events should you attend?
<--- Score

75. What activities does the governance board need to consider?
<--- Score

76. Are your goals realistic? Do you need to redefine your problem? Perhaps the problem has changed or maybe you have reached your goal and need to set a new one?
<--- Score

77. What needs to be done?
<--- Score

78. Are there recognized Applied behavior analysis problems?
<--- Score

79. Are controls defined to recognize and contain problems?

<--- Score

80. What is the recognized need?
<--- Score

81. Who are your key stakeholders who need to sign off?
<--- Score

82. Did you miss any major Applied behavior analysis issues?
<--- Score

83. What situation(s) led to this Applied behavior analysis Self Assessment?
<--- Score

84. Are employees recognized for desired behaviors?
<--- Score

85. How are the Applied behavior analysis's objectives aligned to the group's overall stakeholder strategy?
<--- Score

86. What resources or support might you need?
<--- Score

87. Which issues are too important to ignore?
<--- Score

88. How much are sponsors, customers, partners, stakeholders involved in Applied behavior analysis? In other words, what are the risks, if Applied behavior analysis does not deliver successfully?
<--- Score

89. Consider your own Applied behavior analysis project, what types of organizational problems do you think might be causing or affecting your problem, based on the work done so far?
<--- Score

90. What are the minority interests and what amount of minority interests can be recognized?
<--- Score

91. Who should resolve the Applied behavior analysis issues?
<--- Score

92. Think about the people you identified for your Applied behavior analysis project and the project responsibilities you would assign to them, what kind of training do you think they would need to perform these responsibilities effectively?
<--- Score

93. How do you assess your Applied behavior analysis workforce capability and capacity needs, including skills, competencies, and staffing levels?
<--- Score

94. Who needs to know?
<--- Score

95. Where do you need to exercise leadership?
<--- Score

96. Have you identified your Applied behavior analysis key performance indicators?
<--- Score

Add up total points for this section:
_____ = Total points for this section

Divided by: _____ (number of statements answered) = _____
Average score for this section

Transfer your score to the Applied behavior analysis Index at the beginning of the Self-Assessment.

CRITERION #2: DEFINE:

INTENT: Formulate the stakeholder problem. Define the problem, needs and objectives.

In my belief, the answer to this question is clearly defined:

5 Strongly Agree

4 Agree

3 Neutral

2 Disagree

1 Strongly Disagree

1. Who are the Applied behavior analysis improvement team members, including Management Leads and Coaches?
<--- Score

2. Have specific policy objectives been defined?
<--- Score

3. Is data collected and displayed to better understand

customer(s) critical needs and requirements.
<--- Score

4. What is the scope?
<--- Score

5. Is there any additional Applied behavior analysis definition of success?
<--- Score

6. Will team members perform Applied behavior analysis work when assigned and in a timely fashion?
<--- Score

7. What are the tasks and definitions?
<--- Score

8. What are the dynamics of the communication plan?
<--- Score

9. How do you gather the stories?
<--- Score

10. How can the value of Applied behavior analysis be defined?
<--- Score

11. What Applied behavior analysis requirements should be gathered?
<--- Score

12. Is there a completed, verified, and validated high-level 'as is' (not 'should be' or 'could be') stakeholder process map?
<--- Score

13. What are the Roles and Responsibilities for each team member and its leadership? Where is this documented?

<--- Score

14. What is the definition of Applied behavior analysis excellence?

<--- Score

15. Are there any constraints known that bear on the ability to perform Applied behavior analysis work? How is the team addressing them?

<--- Score

16. What are the compelling stakeholder reasons for embarking on Applied behavior analysis?

<--- Score

17. Has the Applied behavior analysis work been fairly and/or equitably divided and delegated among team members who are qualified and capable to perform the work? Has everyone contributed?

<--- Score

18. What is the definition of success?

<--- Score

19. Is Applied behavior analysis required?

<--- Score

20. How have you defined all Applied behavior analysis requirements first?

<--- Score

21. How do you keep key subject matter experts in the loop?

<--- Score

22. What is out of scope?
<--- Score

23. When are meeting minutes sent out? Who is on the distribution list?
<--- Score

24. Are there different segments of customers?
<--- Score

25. Has the direction changed at all during the course of Applied behavior analysis? If so, when did it change and why?
<--- Score

26. How do you build the right business case?
<--- Score

27. Are accountability and ownership for Applied behavior analysis clearly defined?
<--- Score

28. In what way can you redefine the criteria of choice clients have in your category in your favor?
<--- Score

29. What system do you use for gathering Applied behavior analysis information?
<--- Score

30. If substitutes have been appointed, have they been briefed on the Applied behavior analysis goals and received regular communications as to the progress to date?

<--- Score

31. Is the improvement team aware of the different versions of a process: what they think it is vs. what it actually is vs. what it should be vs. what it could be?
<--- Score

32. What key stakeholder process output measure(s) does Applied behavior analysis leverage and how?
<--- Score

33. What information do you gather?
<--- Score

34. Has your scope been defined?
<--- Score

35. How will variation in the actual durations of each activity be dealt with to ensure that the expected Applied behavior analysis results are met?
<--- Score

36. Who is gathering Applied behavior analysis information?
<--- Score

37. Is full participation by members in regularly held team meetings guaranteed?
<--- Score

38. What sources do you use to gather information for a Applied behavior analysis study?
<--- Score

39. What customer feedback methods were used to solicit their input?

<--- Score

40. Is Applied behavior analysis currently on schedule according to the plan?
<--- Score

41. How did the Applied behavior analysis manager receive input to the development of a Applied behavior analysis improvement plan and the estimated completion dates/times of each activity?
<--- Score

42. How would you define Applied behavior analysis leadership?
<--- Score

43. Who is gathering information?
<--- Score

44. What scope do you want your strategy to cover?
<--- Score

45. Does the team have regular meetings?
<--- Score

46. Are approval levels defined for contracts and supplements to contracts?
<--- Score

47. Are required metrics defined, what are they?
<--- Score

48. What are the rough order estimates on cost savings/opportunities that Applied behavior analysis brings?
<--- Score

49. What is the scope of Applied behavior analysis?
<--- Score

50. Are roles and responsibilities formally defined?
<--- Score

51. Are the Applied behavior analysis requirements testable?
<--- Score

52. Do you have a Applied behavior analysis success story or case study ready to tell and share?
<--- Score

53. How do you gather Applied behavior analysis requirements?
<--- Score

54. How do you think the partners involved in Applied behavior analysis would have defined success?
<--- Score

55. What are the requirements for audit information?
<--- Score

56. How do you hand over Applied behavior analysis context?
<--- Score

57. How do you manage scope?
<--- Score

58. What was the context?
<--- Score

59. Are different versions of process maps needed to account for the different types of inputs?
<--- Score

60. What knowledge or experience is required?
<--- Score

61. Has a Applied behavior analysis requirement not been met?
<--- Score

62. What critical content must be communicated – who, what, when, where, and how?
<--- Score

63. What sort of initial information to gather?
<--- Score

64. Is there a completed SIPOC representation, describing the Suppliers, Inputs, Process, Outputs, and Customers?
<--- Score

65. Is the team formed and are team leaders (Coaches and Management Leads) assigned?
<--- Score

66. How do you manage unclear Applied behavior analysis requirements?
<--- Score

67. What constraints exist that might impact the team?
<--- Score

68. Is it clearly defined in and to your organization

what you do?
<--- Score

69. How was the 'as is' process map developed, reviewed, verified and validated?
<--- Score

70. Are task requirements clearly defined?
<--- Score

71. Is Applied behavior analysis linked to key stakeholder goals and objectives?
<--- Score

72. Is the team equipped with available and reliable resources?
<--- Score

73. What is the scope of the Applied behavior analysis effort?
<--- Score

74. When is the estimated completion date?
<--- Score

75. Is there a clear Applied behavior analysis case definition?
<--- Score

76. Has a high-level 'as is' process map been completed, verified and validated?
<--- Score

77. What is the worst case scenario?
<--- Score

78. Has a project plan, Gantt chart, or similar been developed/completed?
<--- Score

79. Is the current 'as is' process being followed? If not, what are the discrepancies?
<--- Score

80. Is the Applied behavior analysis scope manageable?
<--- Score

81. How do you manage changes in Applied behavior analysis requirements?
<--- Score

82. Is the Applied behavior analysis scope complete and appropriately sized?
<--- Score

83. What defines best in class?
<--- Score

84. Is the scope of Applied behavior analysis defined?
<--- Score

85. Are audit criteria, scope, frequency and methods defined?
<--- Score

86. Do you all define Applied behavior analysis in the same way?
<--- Score

87. The political context: who holds power?
<--- Score

88. When is/was the Applied behavior analysis start date?
<--- Score

89. Do the problem and goal statements meet the SMART criteria (specific, measurable, attainable, relevant, and time-bound)?
<--- Score

90. What information should you gather?
<--- Score

91. What is a worst-case scenario for losses?
<--- Score

92. Will a Applied behavior analysis production readiness review be required?
<--- Score

93. How does the Applied behavior analysis manager ensure against scope creep?
<--- Score

94. How is the team tracking and documenting its work?
<--- Score

95. What is in scope?
<--- Score

96. What are the Applied behavior analysis use cases?
<--- Score

97. Who defines (or who defined) the rules and roles?
<--- Score

98. Have all of the relationships been defined properly?
<--- Score

99. Who approved the Applied behavior analysis scope?
<--- Score

100. What happens if Applied behavior analysis's scope changes?
<--- Score

101. What is the context?
<--- Score

102. How would you define the culture at your organization, how susceptible is it to Applied behavior analysis changes?
<--- Score

103. Are improvement team members fully trained on Applied behavior analysis?
<--- Score

104. What gets examined?
<--- Score

105. Has/have the customer(s) been identified?
<--- Score

106. Have the customer needs been translated into specific, measurable requirements? How?
<--- Score

107. Is scope creep really all bad news?

<--- Score

108. What are the boundaries of the scope? What is in bounds and what is not? What is the start point? What is the stop point?
<--- Score

109. Are customer(s) identified and segmented according to their different needs and requirements?
<--- Score

110. Has anyone else (internal or external to the group) attempted to solve this problem or a similar one before? If so, what knowledge can be leveraged from these previous efforts?
<--- Score

111. Are resources adequate for the scope?
<--- Score

112. What intelligence can you gather?
<--- Score

113. Where can you gather more information?
<--- Score

114. How will the Applied behavior analysis team and the group measure complete success of Applied behavior analysis?
<--- Score

115. Is the team adequately staffed with the desired cross-functionality? If not, what additional resources are available to the team?
<--- Score

116. Is special Applied behavior analysis user knowledge required?
<--- Score

117. Does the scope remain the same?
<--- Score

118. Is there a critical path to deliver Applied behavior analysis results?
<--- Score

119. Are the Applied behavior analysis requirements complete?
<--- Score

120. How do you catch Applied behavior analysis definition inconsistencies?
<--- Score

121. Has everyone on the team, including the team leaders, been properly trained?
<--- Score

122. Will team members regularly document their Applied behavior analysis work?
<--- Score

123. What is out-of-scope initially?
<--- Score

124. Has the improvement team collected the 'voice of the customer' (obtained feedback – qualitative and quantitative)?
<--- Score

125. Is there regularly 100% attendance at the

team meetings? If not, have appointed substitutes attended to preserve cross-functionality and full representation?
<--- Score

126. What would be the goal or target for a Applied behavior analysis's improvement team?
<--- Score

127. Are all requirements met?
<--- Score

128. What are (control) requirements for Applied behavior analysis Information?
<--- Score

129. Is there a Applied behavior analysis management charter, including stakeholder case, problem and goal statements, scope, milestones, roles and responsibilities, communication plan?
<--- Score

130. Has a team charter been developed and communicated?
<--- Score

131. Is the work to date meeting requirements?
<--- Score

132. Why are you doing Applied behavior analysis and what is the scope?
<--- Score

133. What is in the scope and what is not in scope?
<--- Score

134. How often are the team meetings?
<--- Score

135. What are the Applied behavior analysis tasks and definitions?
<--- Score

136. What are the record-keeping requirements of Applied behavior analysis activities?
<--- Score

137. What Applied behavior analysis services do you require?
<--- Score

138. What specifically is the problem? Where does it occur? When does it occur? What is its extent?
<--- Score

Add up total points for this section:
_____ = Total points for this section

Divided by: _____ (number of statements answered) = _____
Average score for this section

Transfer your score to the Applied behavior analysis Index at the beginning of the Self-Assessment.

CRITERION #3: MEASURE:

INTENT: Gather the correct data. Measure the current performance and evolution of the situation.

In my belief, the answer to this question is clearly defined:

5 Strongly Agree

4 Agree

3 Neutral

2 Disagree

1 Strongly Disagree

1. How do you verify the Applied behavior analysis requirements quality?
<--- Score

2. Are supply costs steady or fluctuating?
<--- Score

3. What is your Applied behavior analysis quality cost segregation study?

<--- Score

4. How to cause the change?
<--- Score

5. How do you control the overall costs of your work processes?
<--- Score

6. Which Applied behavior analysis impacts are significant?
<--- Score

7. What is the root cause(s) of the problem?
<--- Score

8. Are you aware of what could cause a problem?
<--- Score

9. What are the Applied behavior analysis investment costs?
<--- Score

10. How do you verify the authenticity of the data and information used?
<--- Score

11. Which measures and indicators matter?
<--- Score

12. Have you included everything in your Applied behavior analysis cost models?
<--- Score

13. How much does it cost?
<--- Score

14. What relevant entities could be measured?
<--- Score

15. What harm might be caused?
<--- Score

16. Are the units of measure consistent?
<--- Score

17. Do you have any cost Applied behavior analysis limitation requirements?
<--- Score

18. What are the operational costs after Applied behavior analysis deployment?
<--- Score

19. How do you measure variability?
<--- Score

20. How can you manage cost down?
<--- Score

21. What are the uncertainties surrounding estimates of impact?
<--- Score

22. Are you able to realize any cost savings?
<--- Score

23. How long to keep data and how to manage retention costs?
<--- Score

24. Is the cost worth the Applied behavior analysis

effort?
<--- Score

25. What is the total fixed cost?
<--- Score

26. What would be a real cause for concern?
<--- Score

27. What potential environmental factors impact the Applied behavior analysis effort?
<--- Score

28. How do you measure lifecycle phases?
<--- Score

29. Is it possible to estimate the impact of unanticipated complexity such as wrong or failed assumptions, feedback, etcetera on proposed reforms?
<--- Score

30. Are there measurements based on task performance?
<--- Score

31. What does losing customers cost your organization?
<--- Score

32. Where is the cost?
<--- Score

33. Do you have a flow diagram of what happens?
<--- Score

34. Why a Applied behavior analysis focus?
<--- Score

35. Do the benefits outweigh the costs?
<--- Score

36. Are the measurements objective?
<--- Score

37. Where is it measured?
<--- Score

38. How can you reduce costs?
<--- Score

39. How frequently do you verify your Applied behavior analysis strategy?
<--- Score

40. Are you taking your company in the direction of better and revenue or cheaper and cost?
<--- Score

41. What is an unallowable cost?
<--- Score

42. What are your customers expectations and measures?
<--- Score

43. How do you verify your resources?
<--- Score

44. What causes extra work or rework?
<--- Score

45. How do you prevent mis-estimating cost?
<--- Score

46. What happens if cost savings do not materialize?
<--- Score

47. What are you verifying?
<--- Score

48. How will effects be measured?
<--- Score

49. How frequently do you track Applied behavior analysis measures?
<--- Score

50. How is performance measured?
<--- Score

51. Are indirect costs charged to the Applied behavior analysis program?
<--- Score

52. What does verifying compliance entail?
<--- Score

53. Did you tackle the cause or the symptom?
<--- Score

54. What does your operating model cost?
<--- Score

55. How do you measure success?
<--- Score

56. Who pays the cost?

<--- Score

57. Are there competing Applied behavior analysis priorities?
<--- Score

58. What are your operating costs?
<--- Score

59. How can a Applied behavior analysis test verify your ideas or assumptions?
<--- Score

60. Are the Applied behavior analysis benefits worth its costs?
<--- Score

61. When should you bother with diagrams?
<--- Score

62. How do you verify Applied behavior analysis completeness and accuracy?
<--- Score

63. What measurements are being captured?
<--- Score

64. What are your key Applied behavior analysis organizational performance measures, including key short and longer-term financial measures?
<--- Score

65. Among the Applied behavior analysis product and service cost to be estimated, which is considered hardest to estimate?
<--- Score

66. What could cause delays in the schedule?
<--- Score

67. When a disaster occurs, who gets priority?
<--- Score

68. What are the costs and benefits?
<--- Score

69. What causes investor action?
<--- Score

70. Who is involved in verifying compliance?
<--- Score

71. What tests verify requirements?
<--- Score

72. What are the strategic priorities for this year?
<--- Score

73. Are missed Applied behavior analysis opportunities costing your organization money?
<--- Score

74. How do you aggregate measures across priorities?
<--- Score

75. What are the costs?
<--- Score

76. Are there any easy-to-implement alternatives to Applied behavior analysis? Sometimes other solutions are available that do not require the cost implications of a full-blown project?

<--- Score

77. What users will be impacted?
<--- Score

78. What methods are feasible and acceptable to estimate the impact of reforms?
<--- Score

79. What are the current costs of the Applied behavior analysis process?
<--- Score

80. What causes mismanagement?
<--- Score

81. How do you measure efficient delivery of Applied behavior analysis services?
<--- Score

82. How is progress measured?
<--- Score

83. How are you verifying it?
<--- Score

84. What drives O&M cost?
<--- Score

85. What is your decision requirements diagram?
<--- Score

86. Do you effectively measure and reward individual and team performance?
<--- Score

87. Does the Applied behavior analysis task fit the client's priorities?
<--- Score

88. Are actual costs in line with budgeted costs?
<--- Score

89. What is the cost of rework?
<--- Score

90. Have you made assumptions about the shape of the future, particularly its impact on your customers and competitors?
<--- Score

91. How do your measurements capture actionable Applied behavior analysis information for use in exceeding your customers expectations and securing your customers engagement?
<--- Score

92. What are allowable costs?
<--- Score

93. What could cause you to change course?
<--- Score

94. What are your primary costs, revenues, assets?
<--- Score

95. How sensitive must the Applied behavior analysis strategy be to cost?
<--- Score

96. Is there an opportunity to verify requirements?
<--- Score

97. What can be used to verify compliance?
<--- Score

98. How is the value delivered by Applied behavior analysis being measured?
<--- Score

99. What are hidden Applied behavior analysis quality costs?
<--- Score

100. What would it cost to replace your technology?
<--- Score

101. Do you verify that corrective actions were taken?
<--- Score

102. How are costs allocated?
<--- Score

103. What does a Test Case verify?
<--- Score

104. How do you stay flexible and focused to recognize larger Applied behavior analysis results?
<--- Score

105. Why do the measurements/indicators matter?
<--- Score

106. How will measures be used to manage and adapt?
<--- Score

107. What measurements are possible, practicable

and meaningful?
<--- Score

108. What are the types and number of measures to use?
<--- Score

109. Who should receive measurement reports?
<--- Score

110. How do you quantify and qualify impacts?
<--- Score

111. What is measured? Why?
<--- Score

112. Do you have an issue in getting priority?
<--- Score

113. How do you verify and validate the Applied behavior analysis data?
<--- Score

114. Will Applied behavior analysis have an impact on current business continuity, disaster recovery processes and/or infrastructure?
<--- Score

115. What disadvantage does this cause for the user?
<--- Score

116. What is the cause of any Applied behavior analysis gaps?
<--- Score

117. Why do you expend time and effort to

implement measurement, for whom?
<--- Score

118. Is the solution cost-effective?
<--- Score

119. How will you measure success?
<--- Score

120. Do you aggressively reward and promote the people who have the biggest impact on creating excellent Applied behavior analysis services/products?
<--- Score

121. What details are required of the Applied behavior analysis cost structure?
<--- Score

122. How do you verify and develop ideas and innovations?
<--- Score

123. Does management have the right priorities among projects?
<--- Score

124. What causes innovation to fail or succeed in your organization?
<--- Score

125. At what cost?
<--- Score

126. How can you reduce the costs of obtaining inputs?

<--- Score

127. Was a business case (cost/benefit) developed?
<--- Score

128. Which costs should be taken into account?
<--- Score

129. What is the Applied behavior analysis business impact?
<--- Score

130. What do people want to verify?
<--- Score

131. How do you verify if Applied behavior analysis is built right?
<--- Score

132. How will costs be allocated?
<--- Score

133. How will you measure your Applied behavior analysis effectiveness?
<--- Score

134. What are the estimated costs of proposed changes?
<--- Score

135. What are the Applied behavior analysis key cost drivers?
<--- Score

136. What is the total cost related to deploying Applied behavior analysis, including any consulting or

professional services?
<--- Score

137. How are measurements made?
<--- Score

138. Where can you go to verify the info?
<--- Score

Add up total points for this section:
_ _ _ _ _ = Total points for this section

Divided by: _ _ _ _ _ _ (number of statements answered) = _ _ _ _ _ _
Average score for this section

Transfer your score to the Applied behavior analysis Index at the beginning of the Self-Assessment.

CRITERION #4: ANALYZE:

INTENT: Analyze causes, assumptions and hypotheses.

In my belief, the answer to this question is clearly defined:

5 Strongly Agree

4 Agree

3 Neutral

2 Disagree

1 Strongly Disagree

1. Do your contracts/agreements contain data security obligations?
<--- Score

2. What are your key performance measures or indicators and in-process measures for the control and improvement of your Applied behavior analysis processes?
<--- Score

3. How do you define collaboration and team output?
<--- Score

4. How is the Applied behavior analysis Value Stream Mapping managed?
<--- Score

5. Did any value-added analysis or 'lean thinking' take place to identify some of the gaps shown on the 'as is' process map?
<--- Score

6. How was the detailed process map generated, verified, and validated?
<--- Score

7. When should a process be art not science?
<--- Score

8. How will the data be checked for quality?
<--- Score

9. Is the final output clearly identified?
<--- Score

10. Do staff qualifications match your project?
<--- Score

11. What controls do you have in place to protect data?
<--- Score

12. What output to create?
<--- Score

13. How has the Applied behavior analysis data been

gathered?
<--- Score

14. What training and qualifications will you need?
<--- Score

15. What were the financial benefits resulting from any 'ground fruit or low-hanging fruit' (quick fixes)?
<--- Score

16. Who owns what data?
<--- Score

17. Is pre-qualification of suppliers carried out?
<--- Score

18. Who gets your output?
<--- Score

19. Is data and process analysis, root cause analysis and quantifying the gap/opportunity in place?
<--- Score

20. What are your current levels and trends in key Applied behavior analysis measures or indicators of product and process performance that are important to and directly serve your customers?
<--- Score

21. What Applied behavior analysis data should be managed?
<--- Score

22. Can you add value to the current Applied behavior analysis decision-making process (largely qualitative) by incorporating uncertainty modeling (more

quantitative)?
<--- Score

23. What, related to, Applied behavior analysis processes does your organization outsource?
<--- Score

24. What process should you select for improvement?
<--- Score

25. Are you missing Applied behavior analysis opportunities?
<--- Score

26. Who will facilitate the team and process?
<--- Score

27. What are evaluation criteria for the output?
<--- Score

28. Is the suppliers process defined and controlled?
<--- Score

29. Were there any improvement opportunities identified from the process analysis?
<--- Score

30. How do you use Applied behavior analysis data and information to support organizational decision making and innovation?
<--- Score

31. What tools were used to narrow the list of possible causes?
<--- Score

32. What Applied behavior analysis data should be collected?
<--- Score

33. What internal processes need improvement?
<--- Score

34. What qualifications and skills do you need?
<--- Score

35. How is the data gathered?
<--- Score

36. What do you need to qualify?
<--- Score

37. Is the performance gap determined?
<--- Score

38. What successful thing are you doing today that may be blinding you to new growth opportunities?
<--- Score

39. How do you promote understanding that opportunity for improvement is not criticism of the status quo, or the people who created the status quo?
<--- Score

40. What is the oversight process?
<--- Score

41. Are Applied behavior analysis changes recognized early enough to be approved through the regular process?
<--- Score

42. How do you identify specific Applied behavior analysis investment opportunities and emerging trends?
<--- Score

43. What kind of crime could a potential new hire have committed that would not only not disqualify him/her from being hired by your organization, but would actually indicate that he/she might be a particularly good fit?
<--- Score

44. How difficult is it to qualify what Applied behavior analysis ROI is?
<--- Score

45. What is the Applied behavior analysis Driver?
<--- Score

46. How will the change process be managed?
<--- Score

47. How will corresponding data be collected?
<--- Score

48. What are the Applied behavior analysis design outputs?
<--- Score

49. What information qualified as important?
<--- Score

50. Where can you get qualified talent today?
<--- Score

51. What conclusions were drawn from the team's

data collection and analysis? How did the team reach these conclusions?
<--- Score

52. Who will gather what data?
<--- Score

53. How often will data be collected for measures?
<--- Score

54. What qualifies as competition?
<--- Score

55. Where is Applied behavior analysis data gathered?
<--- Score

56. Record-keeping requirements flow from the records needed as inputs, outputs, controls and for transformation of a Applied behavior analysis process, are the records needed as inputs to the Applied behavior analysis process available?
<--- Score

57. Think about the functions involved in your Applied behavior analysis project, what processes flow from these functions?
<--- Score

58. What qualifications are necessary?
<--- Score

59. Is there a strict change management process?
<--- Score

60. Have the problem and goal statements been updated to reflect the additional knowledge gained

from the analyze phase?
<--- Score

61. What are the disruptive Applied behavior analysis technologies that enable your organization to radically change your business processes?
<--- Score

62. Do you, as a leader, bounce back quickly from setbacks?
<--- Score

63. How can risk management be tied procedurally to process elements?
<--- Score

64. How are outputs preserved and protected?
<--- Score

65. What qualifications are needed?
<--- Score

66. A compounding model resolution with available relevant data can often provide insight towards a solution methodology; which Applied behavior analysis models, tools and techniques are necessary?
<--- Score

67. How do mission and objectives affect the Applied behavior analysis processes of your organization?
<--- Score

68. What Applied behavior analysis metrics are outputs of the process?
<--- Score

69. How is Applied behavior analysis data gathered?
<--- Score

70. Is the gap/opportunity displayed and communicated in financial terms?
<--- Score

71. What does the data say about the performance of the stakeholder process?
<--- Score

72. Do several people in different organizational units assist with the Applied behavior analysis process?
<--- Score

73. What is the complexity of the output produced?
<--- Score

74. Are all staff in core Applied behavior analysis subjects Highly Qualified?
<--- Score

75. Are all team members qualified for all tasks?
<--- Score

76. What process improvements will be needed?
<--- Score

77. What Applied behavior analysis data do you gather or use now?
<--- Score

78. Which Applied behavior analysis data should be retained?
<--- Score

79. Think about some of the processes you undertake within your organization, which do you own?
<--- Score

80. Was a cause-and-effect diagram used to explore the different types of causes (or sources of variation)?
<--- Score

81. What is the Value Stream Mapping?
<--- Score

82. Should you invest in industry-recognized qualifications?
<--- Score

83. Have you defined which data is gathered how?
<--- Score

84. What methods do you use to gather Applied behavior analysis data?
<--- Score

85. What are the personnel training and qualifications required?
<--- Score

86. Do your employees have the opportunity to do what they do best everyday?
<--- Score

87. Who is involved in the management review process?
<--- Score

88. How much data can be collected in the given timeframe?

<--- Score

89. What types of data do your Applied behavior analysis indicators require?
<--- Score

90. Are your outputs consistent?
<--- Score

91. How do your work systems and key work processes relate to and capitalize on your core competencies?
<--- Score

92. Where is the data coming from to measure compliance?
<--- Score

93. What are your Applied behavior analysis processes?
<--- Score

94. Is the required Applied behavior analysis data gathered?
<--- Score

95. How many input/output points does it require?
<--- Score

96. What are the processes for audit reporting and management?
<--- Score

97. What is the output?
<--- Score

98. What are your outputs?
<--- Score

99. Were Pareto charts (or similar) used to portray the 'heavy hitters' (or key sources of variation)?
<--- Score

100. Was a detailed process map created to amplify critical steps of the 'as is' stakeholder process?
<--- Score

101. What is the cost of poor quality as supported by the team's analysis?
<--- Score

102. Do you have the authority to produce the output?
<--- Score

103. What are the revised rough estimates of the financial savings/opportunity for Applied behavior analysis improvements?
<--- Score

104. Have any additional benefits been identified that will result from closing all or most of the gaps?
<--- Score

105. What quality tools were used to get through the analyze phase?
<--- Score

106. What is your organizations system for selecting qualified vendors?
<--- Score

107. How will the Applied behavior analysis data be captured?
<--- Score

108. Is there an established change management process?
<--- Score

109. Were any designed experiments used to generate additional insight into the data analysis?
<--- Score

110. Who is involved with workflow mapping?
<--- Score

111. What resources go in to get the desired output?
<--- Score

112. An organizationally feasible system request is one that considers the mission, goals and objectives of the organization, key questions are: is the Applied behavior analysis solution request practical and will it solve a problem or take advantage of an opportunity to achieve company goals?
<--- Score

113. What Applied behavior analysis data will be collected?
<--- Score

114. How is data used for program management and improvement?
<--- Score

115. What are your current levels and trends in key measures or indicators of Applied behavior analysis

product and process performance that are important to and directly serve your customers? How do these results compare with the performance of your competitors and other organizations with similar offerings?
<--- Score

116. How do you measure the operational performance of your key work systems and processes, including productivity, cycle time, and other appropriate measures of process effectiveness, efficiency, and innovation?
<--- Score

117. How does the organization define, manage, and improve its Applied behavior analysis processes?
<--- Score

118. Do quality systems drive continuous improvement?
<--- Score

119. Has data output been validated?
<--- Score

120. What systems/processes must you excel at?
<--- Score

121. What did the team gain from developing a sub-process map?
<--- Score

122. What is your organizations process which leads to recognition of value generation?
<--- Score

123. How do you implement and manage your work processes to ensure that they meet design requirements?

<--- Score

124. Has an output goal been set?

<--- Score

125. What other organizational variables, such as reward systems or communication systems, affect the performance of this Applied behavior analysis process?

<--- Score

126. Do your leaders quickly bounce back from setbacks?

<--- Score

127. What are the necessary qualifications?

<--- Score

128. What tools were used to generate the list of possible causes?

<--- Score

129. Do you understand your management processes today?

<--- Score

130. What were the crucial 'moments of truth' on the process map?

<--- Score

131. How is the way you as the leader think and process information affecting your organizational culture?

<--- Score

132. Is the Applied behavior analysis process severely broken such that a re-design is necessary?
<--- Score

133. What are the Applied behavior analysis business drivers?
<--- Score

134. Is there any way to speed up the process?
<--- Score

135. What data is gathered?
<--- Score

136. Who qualifies to gain access to data?
<--- Score

Add up total points for this section:
_____ = Total points for this section

Divided by: _____ (number of statements answered) = _____
Average score for this section

Transfer your score to the Applied behavior analysis Index at the beginning of the Self-Assessment.

CRITERION #5: IMPROVE:

INTENT: Develop a practical solution. Innovate, establish and test the solution and to measure the results.

In my belief, the answer to this question is clearly defined:

5 Strongly Agree

4 Agree

3 Neutral

2 Disagree

1 Strongly Disagree

1. What improvements have been achieved?
<--- Score

2. Do you need to do a usability evaluation?
<--- Score

3. How do you improve your likelihood of success ?
<--- Score

4. How is continuous improvement applied to risk management?
<--- Score

5. What tools do you use once you have decided on a Applied behavior analysis strategy and more importantly how do you choose?
<--- Score

6. What are the Applied behavior analysis security risks?
<--- Score

7. How do you go about comparing Applied behavior analysis approaches/solutions?
<--- Score

8. Risk Identification: What are the possible risk events your organization faces in relation to Applied behavior analysis?
<--- Score

9. What are the concrete Applied behavior analysis results?
<--- Score

10. Are you assessing Applied behavior analysis and risk?
<--- Score

11. What is the implementation plan?
<--- Score

12. Is the solution technically practical?
<--- Score

13. Risk factors: what are the characteristics of Applied behavior analysis that make it risky?
<--- Score

14. How will you measure the results?
<--- Score

15. What alternative responses are available to manage risk?
<--- Score

16. Who will be responsible for making the decisions to include or exclude requested changes once Applied behavior analysis is underway?
<--- Score

17. How do you improve productivity?
<--- Score

18. How can you improve performance?
<--- Score

19. What does the 'should be' process map/design look like?
<--- Score

20. What to do with the results or outcomes of measurements?
<--- Score

21. What are the affordable Applied behavior analysis risks?
<--- Score

22. How will you know that you have improved?
<--- Score

23. Who do you report Applied behavior analysis results to?
<--- Score

24. What should a proof of concept or pilot accomplish?
<--- Score

25. How can skill-level changes improve Applied behavior analysis?
<--- Score

26. Do vendor agreements bring new compliance risk ?
<--- Score

27. How does the team improve its work?
<--- Score

28. Are risk management tasks balanced centrally and locally?
<--- Score

29. Is the Applied behavior analysis risk managed?
<--- Score

30. What is the risk?
<--- Score

31. Who manages supplier risk management in your organization?
<--- Score

32. How do you keep improving Applied behavior analysis?

<--- Score

33. What risks do you need to manage?
<--- Score

34. How do you link measurement and risk?
<--- Score

35. Do you have the optimal project management team structure?
<--- Score

36. Is any Applied behavior analysis documentation required?
<--- Score

37. Are procedures documented for managing Applied behavior analysis risks?
<--- Score

38. What can you do to improve?
<--- Score

39. Can the solution be designed and implemented within an acceptable time period?
<--- Score

40. How do you define the solutions' scope?
<--- Score

41. Who are the key stakeholders for the Applied behavior analysis evaluation?
<--- Score

42. How will you know that a change is an improvement?

<--- Score

43. For decision problems, how do you develop a decision statement?
<--- Score

44. Can you integrate quality management and risk management?
<--- Score

45. Is there a high likelihood that any recommendations will achieve their intended results?
<--- Score

46. What Applied behavior analysis improvements can be made?
<--- Score

47. Is there any other Applied behavior analysis solution?
<--- Score

48. What area needs the greatest improvement?
<--- Score

49. Are risk triggers captured?
<--- Score

50. What do you want to improve?
<--- Score

51. Was a Applied behavior analysis charter developed?
<--- Score

52. How can you better manage risk?

<--- Score

53. What resources are required for the improvement efforts?
<--- Score

54. How is knowledge sharing about risk management improved?
<--- Score

55. Is the measure of success for Applied behavior analysis understandable to a variety of people?
<--- Score

56. How are policy decisions made and where?
<--- Score

57. Who will be using the results of the measurement activities?
<--- Score

58. What is the magnitude of the improvements?
<--- Score

59. Which Applied behavior analysis solution is appropriate?
<--- Score

60. Why improve in the first place?
<--- Score

61. Are events managed to resolution?
<--- Score

62. What are your current levels and trends in key measures or indicators of workforce and leader

development?
<--- Score

63. Does the goal represent a desired result that can be measured?
<--- Score

64. How do you manage Applied behavior analysis risk?
<--- Score

65. What assumptions are made about the solution and approach?
<--- Score

66. What is Applied behavior analysis's impact on utilizing the best solution(s)?
<--- Score

67. What are the implications of the one critical Applied behavior analysis decision 10 minutes, 10 months, and 10 years from now?
<--- Score

68. Are the key business and technology risks being managed?
<--- Score

69. Do those selected for the Applied behavior analysis team have a good general understanding of what Applied behavior analysis is all about?
<--- Score

70. Applied behavior analysis risk decisions: whose call Is It?
<--- Score

71. How do you decide how much to remunerate an employee?//
<--- Score

72. How do you manage and improve your Applied behavior analysis work systems to deliver customer value and achieve organizational success and sustainability?
<--- Score

73. What criteria will you use to assess your Applied behavior analysis risks?
<--- Score

74. Where do the Applied behavior analysis decisions reside?
<--- Score

75. What are the expected Applied behavior analysis results?
<--- Score

76. What went well, what should change, what can improve?
<--- Score

77. Have you identified breakpoints and/or risk tolerances that will trigger broad consideration of a potential need for intervention or modification of strategy?
<--- Score

78. Do you combine technical expertise with business knowledge and Applied behavior analysis Key topics include lifecycles, development approaches,

requirements and how to make a business case?
<--- Score

79. How can you improve Applied behavior analysis?
<--- Score

80. What practices helps your organization to develop its capacity to recognize patterns?
<--- Score

81. Which of the recognised risks out of all risks can be most likely transferred?
<--- Score

82. How do you mitigate Applied behavior analysis risk?
<--- Score

83. What tools were most useful during the improve phase?
<--- Score

84. How risky is your organization?
<--- Score

85. How do you deal with Applied behavior analysis risk?
<--- Score

86. What were the underlying assumptions on the cost-benefit analysis?
<--- Score

87. Do you cover the five essential competencies: Communication, Collaboration,Innovation, Adaptability, and Leadership that improve an

organizations ability to leverage the new Applied behavior analysis in a volatile global economy?
<--- Score

88. What is the team's contingency plan for potential problems occurring in implementation?
<--- Score

89. Is the scope clearly documented?
<--- Score

90. What current systems have to be understood and/or changed?
<--- Score

91. Is the Applied behavior analysis solution sustainable?
<--- Score

92. What actually has to improve and by how much?
<--- Score

93. Is risk periodically assessed?
<--- Score

94. Would you develop a Applied behavior analysis Communication Strategy?
<--- Score

95. What is Applied behavior analysis risk?
<--- Score

96. Are the most efficient solutions problem-specific?
<--- Score

97. Has reinforcement for absence of the behavior

been systematically evaluated?
<--- Score

98. What is the Applied behavior analysis's sustainability risk?
<--- Score

99. Who are the Applied behavior analysis decision-makers?
<--- Score

100. In the past few months, what is the smallest change you have made that has had the biggest positive result? What was it about that small change that produced the large return?
<--- Score

101. How can the phases of Applied behavior analysis development be identified?
<--- Score

102. Risk events: what are the things that could go wrong?
<--- Score

103. What tools were used to evaluate the potential solutions?
<--- Score

104. At what point will vulnerability assessments be performed once Applied behavior analysis is put into production (e.g., ongoing Risk Management after implementation)?
<--- Score

105. Have you achieved Applied behavior analysis

improvements?
<--- Score

106. How do the Applied behavior analysis results compare with the performance of your competitors and other organizations with similar offerings?
<--- Score

107. Who are the people involved in developing and implementing Applied behavior analysis?
<--- Score

108. What were the criteria for evaluating a Applied behavior analysis pilot?
<--- Score

109. How scalable is your Applied behavior analysis solution?
<--- Score

110. How do you measure risk?
<--- Score

111. Who are the Applied behavior analysis decision makers?
<--- Score

112. Who manages Applied behavior analysis risk?
<--- Score

113. Can you identify any significant risks or exposures to Applied behavior analysis third- parties (vendors, service providers, alliance partners etc) that concern you?
<--- Score

114. Where do you need Applied behavior analysis improvement?
<--- Score

115. Who will be responsible for documenting the Applied behavior analysis requirements in detail?
<--- Score

116. How will you know when its improved?
<--- Score

117. Is the Applied behavior analysis documentation thorough?
<--- Score

118. Who should make the Applied behavior analysis decisions?
<--- Score

119. When you map the key players in your own work and the types/domains of relationships with them, which relationships do you find easy and which challenging, and why?
<--- Score

120. What tools were used to tap into the creativity and encourage 'outside the box' thinking?
<--- Score

121. Does a good decision guarantee a good outcome?
<--- Score

122. To what extent does management recognize Applied behavior analysis as a tool to increase the results?

<--- Score

123. How are Applied behavior analysis risks managed?
<--- Score

124. What lessons, if any, from a pilot were incorporated into the design of the full-scale solution?
<--- Score

125. Is Applied behavior analysis documentation maintained?
<--- Score

126. Are the risks fully understood, reasonable and manageable?
<--- Score

127. What needs improvement? Why?
<--- Score

128. What error proofing will be done to address some of the discrepancies observed in the 'as is' process?
<--- Score

129. Who makes the Applied behavior analysis decisions in your organization?
<--- Score

130. Explorations of the frontiers of Applied behavior analysis will help you build influence, improve Applied behavior analysis, optimize decision making, and sustain change, what is your approach?
<--- Score

131. How do you measure improved Applied behavior

analysis service perception, and satisfaction?
<--- Score

132. How significant is the improvement in the eyes of the end user?
<--- Score

133. Will the controls trigger any other risks?
<--- Score

134. Is supporting Applied behavior analysis documentation required?
<--- Score

Add up total points for this section:
_____ = Total points for this section

Divided by: _____ (number of statements answered) = _____
Average score for this section

Transfer your score to the Applied behavior analysis Index at the beginning of the Self-Assessment.

CRITERION #6: CONTROL:

INTENT: Implement the practical solution. Maintain the performance and correct possible complications.

In my belief, the answer to this question is clearly defined:

5 Strongly Agree

4 Agree

3 Neutral

2 Disagree

1 Strongly Disagree

1. Are you measuring, monitoring and predicting Applied behavior analysis activities to optimize operations and profitability, and enhancing outcomes?
<--- Score

2. Are pertinent alerts monitored, analyzed and distributed to appropriate personnel?
<--- Score

3. What quality tools were useful in the control phase?
<--- Score

4. Are suggested corrective/restorative actions indicated on the response plan for known causes to problems that might surface?
<--- Score

5. How do you spread information?
<--- Score

6. What are the critical parameters to watch?
<--- Score

7. What is your theory of human motivation, and how does your compensation plan fit with that view?
<--- Score

8. Who sets the Applied behavior analysis standards?
<--- Score

9. Implementation Planning: is a pilot needed to test the changes before a full roll out occurs?
<--- Score

10. Are operating procedures consistent?
<--- Score

11. Is there a documented and implemented monitoring plan?
<--- Score

12. What are you attempting to measure/monitor?
<--- Score

13. How will the process owner and team be able to hold the gains?
<--- Score

14. In the case of a Applied behavior analysis project, the criteria for the audit derive from implementation objectives, an audit of a Applied behavior analysis project involves assessing whether the recommendations outlined for implementation have been met, can you track that any Applied behavior analysis project is implemented as planned, and is it working?
<--- Score

15. What are customers monitoring?
<--- Score

16. What are the key elements of your Applied behavior analysis performance improvement system, including your evaluation, organizational learning, and innovation processes?
<--- Score

17. Will any special training be provided for results interpretation?
<--- Score

18. Has the improved process and its steps been standardized?
<--- Score

19. Does the response plan contain a definite closed loop continual improvement scheme (e.g., plan-do-check-act)?
<--- Score

20. What is the recommended frequency of auditing?
<--- Score

21. How do senior leaders actions reflect a commitment to the organizations Applied behavior analysis values?
<--- Score

22. How will input, process, and output variables be checked to detect for sub-optimal conditions?
<--- Score

23. What are the performance and scale of the Applied behavior analysis tools?
<--- Score

24. Is new knowledge gained imbedded in the response plan?
<--- Score

25. What are the known security controls?
<--- Score

26. How do your controls stack up?
<--- Score

27. Is there a control plan in place for sustaining improvements (short and long-term)?
<--- Score

28. Is there a transfer of ownership and knowledge to process owner and process team tasked with the responsibilities.
<--- Score

29. Do you monitor the Applied behavior analysis

decisions made and fine tune them as they evolve?
<--- Score

30. Have new or revised work instructions resulted?
<--- Score

31. How do you plan for the cost of succession?
<--- Score

32. Are controls in place and consistently applied?
<--- Score

33. Who controls critical resources?
<--- Score

34. Is a response plan established and deployed?
<--- Score

35. Can support from partners be adjusted?
<--- Score

36. Is there a Applied behavior analysis Communication plan covering who needs to get what information when?
<--- Score

37. How do you establish and deploy modified action plans if circumstances require a shift in plans and rapid execution of new plans?
<--- Score

38. Is reporting being used or needed?
<--- Score

39. What do you measure to verify effectiveness gains?

<--- Score

40. What key inputs and outputs are being measured on an ongoing basis?
<--- Score

41. Will the team be available to assist members in planning investigations?
<--- Score

42. Are the planned controls working?
<--- Score

43. Is knowledge gained on process shared and institutionalized?
<--- Score

44. What other systems, operations, processes, and infrastructures (hiring practices, staffing, training, incentives/rewards, metrics/dashboards/scorecards, etc.) need updates, additions, changes, or deletions in order to facilitate knowledge transfer and improvements?
<--- Score

45. How might the group capture best practices and lessons learned so as to leverage improvements?
<--- Score

46. Who is going to spread your message?
<--- Score

47. How is change control managed?
<--- Score

48. How do controls support value?

<--- Score

49. Are new process steps, standards, and documentation ingrained into normal operations?
<--- Score

50. Where do ideas that reach policy makers and planners as proposals for Applied behavior analysis strengthening and reform actually originate?
<--- Score

51. Is there a standardized process?
<--- Score

52. How will you measure your QA plan's effectiveness?
<--- Score

53. How can you best use all of your knowledge repositories to enhance learning and sharing?
<--- Score

54. Are the planned controls in place?
<--- Score

55. What should the next improvement project be that is related to Applied behavior analysis?
<--- Score

56. Will existing staff require re-training, for example, to learn new business processes?
<--- Score

57. Is there an action plan in case of emergencies?
<--- Score

58. How will Applied behavior analysis decisions be made and monitored?
<--- Score

59. Is the Applied behavior analysis test/monitoring cost justified?
<--- Score

60. How will the day-to-day responsibilities for monitoring and continual improvement be transferred from the improvement team to the process owner?
<--- Score

61. Does the Applied behavior analysis performance meet the customer's requirements?
<--- Score

62. Who has control over resources?
<--- Score

63. Do the viable solutions scale to future needs?
<--- Score

64. Is there a recommended audit plan for routine surveillance inspections of Applied behavior analysis's gains?
<--- Score

65. How is Applied behavior analysis project cost planned, managed, monitored?
<--- Score

66. How do you select, collect, align, and integrate Applied behavior analysis data and information for tracking daily operations and overall organizational

performance, including progress relative to strategic objectives and action plans?

<--- Score

67. What can you control?

<--- Score

68. Who is the Applied behavior analysis process owner?

<--- Score

69. Who will be in control?

<--- Score

70. How do you monitor usage and cost?

<--- Score

71. Has the Applied behavior analysis value of standards been quantified?

<--- Score

72. What is your plan to assess your security risks?

<--- Score

73. Are documented procedures clear and easy to follow for the operators?

<--- Score

74. How will the process owner verify improvement in present and future sigma levels, process capabilities?

<--- Score

75. Will your goals reflect your program budget?

<--- Score

76. How widespread is its use?

<--- Score

77. You may have created your quality measures at a time when you lacked resources, technology wasn't up to the required standard, or low service levels were the industry norm. Have those circumstances changed?
<--- Score

78. Are there documented procedures?
<--- Score

79. Does job training on the documented procedures need to be part of the process team's education and training?
<--- Score

80. How do you plan on providing proper recognition and disclosure of supporting companies?
<--- Score

81. Is a response plan in place for when the input, process, or output measures indicate an 'out-of-control' condition?
<--- Score

82. Do you monitor the effectiveness of your Applied behavior analysis activities?
<--- Score

83. What are your results for key measures or indicators of the accomplishment of your Applied behavior analysis strategy and action plans, including building and strengthening core competencies?
<--- Score

84. Is there documentation that will support the successful operation of the improvement?
<--- Score

85. What do you stand for--and what are you against?
<--- Score

86. How will report readings be checked to effectively monitor performance?
<--- Score

87. Can you adapt and adjust to changing Applied behavior analysis situations?
<--- Score

88. How will new or emerging customer needs/requirements be checked/communicated to orient the process toward meeting the new specifications and continually reducing variation?
<--- Score

89. Do the Applied behavior analysis decisions you make today help people and the planet tomorrow?
<--- Score

90. What should you measure to verify efficiency gains?
<--- Score

91. What is the standard for acceptable Applied behavior analysis performance?
<--- Score

92. Against what alternative is success being measured?
<--- Score

93. What is the control/monitoring plan?
<--- Score

94. Are the Applied behavior analysis standards challenging?
<--- Score

95. What other areas of the group might benefit from the Applied behavior analysis team's improvements, knowledge, and learning?
<--- Score

96. Does a troubleshooting guide exist or is it needed?
<--- Score

97. What do your reports reflect?
<--- Score

Add up total points for this section:
_____ = Total points for this section

Divided by: _____ (number of statements answered) = _____
Average score for this section

Transfer your score to the Applied behavior analysis Index at the beginning of the Self-Assessment.

CRITERION #7: SUSTAIN:

INTENT: Retain the benefits.

In my belief, the answer to this question is clearly defined:

5 Strongly Agree

4 Agree

3 Neutral

2 Disagree

1 Strongly Disagree

1. Why is it important to have senior management support for a Applied behavior analysis project?
<--- Score

2. What is your formula for success in Applied behavior analysis ?
<--- Score

3. Think of your Applied behavior analysis project, what are the main functions?
<--- Score

4. How do you make it meaningful in connecting Applied behavior analysis with what users do day-to-day?

<--- Score

5. Who do you want your customers to become?

<--- Score

6. Who do you think the world wants your organization to be?

<--- Score

7. How do you ensure that implementations of Applied behavior analysis products are done in a way that ensures safety?

<--- Score

8. What is your Applied behavior analysis strategy?

<--- Score

9. Are your responses positive or negative?

<--- Score

10. What trophy do you want on your mantle?

<--- Score

11. Have benefits been optimized with all key stakeholders?

<--- Score

12. What management system can you use to leverage the Applied behavior analysis experience, ideas, and concerns of the people closest to the work to be done?

<--- Score

13. What is your question? Why?
<--- Score

14. How do customers see your organization?
<--- Score

15. Will there be any necessary staff changes (redundancies or new hires)?
<--- Score

16. What is it like to work for you?
<--- Score

17. At what moment would you think; Will I get fired?
<--- Score

18. How long will it take to change?
<--- Score

19. How do you track customer value, profitability or financial return, organizational success, and sustainability?
<--- Score

20. What are specific Applied behavior analysis rules to follow?
<--- Score

21. How do you cross-sell and up-sell your Applied behavior analysis success?
<--- Score

22. What new services of functionality will be implemented next with Applied behavior analysis ?
<--- Score

23. How do you create buy-in?
<--- Score

24. What are your most important goals for the strategic Applied behavior analysis objectives?
<--- Score

25. What will be the consequences to the stakeholder (financial, reputation etc) if Applied behavior analysis does not go ahead or fails to deliver the objectives?
<--- Score

26. Who is responsible for errors?
<--- Score

27. What are the barriers to increased Applied behavior analysis production?
<--- Score

28. How do you lead with Applied behavior analysis in mind?
<--- Score

29. What would have to be true for the option on the table to be the best possible choice?
<--- Score

30. Are the criteria for selecting recommendations stated?
<--- Score

31. What is your competitive advantage?
<--- Score

32. How much contingency will be available in the

budget?
<--- Score

33. Is your strategy driving your strategy? Or is the way in which you allocate resources driving your strategy?
<--- Score

34. How do you accomplish your long range Applied behavior analysis goals?
<--- Score

35. What is an unauthorized commitment?
<--- Score

36. Whose voice (department, ethnic group, women, older workers, etc) might you have missed hearing from in your company, and how might you amplify this voice to create positive momentum for your business?
<--- Score

37. Which individuals, teams or departments will be involved in Applied behavior analysis?
<--- Score

38. What are strategies for increasing support and reducing opposition?
<--- Score

39. Who are your customers?
<--- Score

40. What goals did you miss?
<--- Score

41. What are internal and external Applied behavior analysis relations?
<--- Score

42. Which functions and people interact with the supplier and or customer?
<--- Score

43. Are you paying enough attention to the partners your company depends on to succeed?
<--- Score

44. How will you motivate the stakeholders with the least vested interest?
<--- Score

45. What is something you believe that nearly no one agrees with you on?
<--- Score

46. Who is on the team?
<--- Score

47. Political -is anyone trying to undermine this project?
<--- Score

48. Are there any activities that you can take off your to do list?
<--- Score

49. What trouble can you get into?
<--- Score

50. Marketing budgets are tighter, consumers are more skeptical, and social media has changed forever

the way we talk about Applied behavior analysis, how do you gain traction?
<--- Score

51. Will it be accepted by users?
<--- Score

52. What is effective Applied behavior analysis?
<--- Score

53. What would you recommend your friend do if he/she were facing this dilemma?
<--- Score

54. Did your employees make progress today?
<--- Score

55. How do you maintain Applied behavior analysis's Integrity?
<--- Score

56. What Applied behavior analysis skills are most important?
<--- Score

57. What threat is Applied behavior analysis addressing?
<--- Score

58. If you do not follow, then how to lead?
<--- Score

59. How do you listen to customers to obtain actionable information?
<--- Score

60. What are the key enablers to make this Applied behavior analysis move?
<--- Score

61. What Applied behavior analysis modifications can you make work for you?
<--- Score

62. What is the funding source for this project?
<--- Score

63. What should you stop doing?
<--- Score

64. Who is the main stakeholder, with ultimate responsibility for driving Applied behavior analysis forward?
<--- Score

65. Do you know what you are doing? And who do you call if you don't?
<--- Score

66. What are you challenging?
<--- Score

67. If your customer were your grandmother, would you tell her to buy what you're selling?
<--- Score

68. What are the gaps in your knowledge and experience?
<--- Score

69. Are you changing as fast as the world around you?
<--- Score

70. What are the short and long-term Applied behavior analysis goals?
<--- Score

71. Do you have past Applied behavior analysis successes?
<--- Score

72. How can you become the company that would put you out of business?
<--- Score

73. Are assumptions made in Applied behavior analysis stated explicitly?
<--- Score

74. What unique value proposition (UVP) do you offer?
<--- Score

75. What does your signature ensure?
<--- Score

76. How do you change your name, address and/or contact information?
<--- Score

77. Who is responsible for ensuring appropriate resources (time, people and money) are allocated to Applied behavior analysis?
<--- Score

78. Where can you break convention?
<--- Score

79. Is the Applied behavior analysis organization

completing tasks effectively and efficiently?
<--- Score

80. Why will customers want to buy your organizations products/services?
<--- Score

81. Why not do Applied behavior analysis?
<--- Score

82. Do you think Applied behavior analysis accomplishes the goals you expect it to accomplish?
<--- Score

83. Who will be responsible for deciding whether Applied behavior analysis goes ahead or not after the initial investigations?
<--- Score

84. How does Applied behavior analysis integrate with other stakeholder initiatives?
<--- Score

85. Is it economical; do you have the time and money?
<--- Score

86. How do you contact a board member for information?
<--- Score

87. What is the source of the strategies for Applied behavior analysis strengthening and reform?
<--- Score

88. How do you keep the momentum going?
<--- Score

89. What must you excel at?
<--- Score

90. Would you rather sell to knowledgeable and informed customers or to uninformed customers?
<--- Score

91. What do we do when new problems arise?
<--- Score

92. In a project to restructure Applied behavior analysis outcomes, which stakeholders would you involve?
<--- Score

93. Is there a work around that you can use?
<--- Score

94. How do you provide a safe environment -physically and emotionally?
<--- Score

95. What are you trying to prove to yourself, and how might it be hijacking your life and business success?
<--- Score

96. How will you insure seamless interoperability of Applied behavior analysis moving forward?
<--- Score

97. How do you determine the key elements that affect Applied behavior analysis workforce satisfaction, how are these elements determined for different workforce groups and segments?
<--- Score

98. What information is critical to your organization that your executives are ignoring?
<--- Score

99. Has implementation been effective in reaching specified objectives so far?
<--- Score

100. What may be the consequences for the performance of an organization if all stakeholders are not consulted regarding Applied behavior analysis?
<--- Score

101. How is implementation research currently incorporated into each of your goals?
<--- Score

102. What counts that you are not counting?
<--- Score

103. How do you know if you are successful?
<--- Score

104. Who uses your product in ways you never expected?
<--- Score

105. What is organizational performance engineering?
<--- Score

106. Are you using a design thinking approach and integrating Innovation, Applied behavior analysis Experience, and Brand Value?
<--- Score

107. What is the range of capabilities?
<--- Score

108. What are the essentials of internal Applied behavior analysis management?
<--- Score

109. Can you break it down?
<--- Score

110. What is the craziest thing you can do?
<--- Score

111. Can you do all this work?
<--- Score

112. Is maximizing Applied behavior analysis protection the same as minimizing Applied behavior analysis loss?
<--- Score

113. Do Applied behavior analysis rules make a reasonable demand on a users capabilities?
<--- Score

114. What have been your experiences in defining long range Applied behavior analysis goals?
<--- Score

115. What happens at your organization when people fail?
<--- Score

116. Are you maintaining a past–present–future perspective throughout the Applied behavior analysis

discussion?
<--- Score

117. Are you making progress, and are you making progress as Applied behavior analysis leaders?
<--- Score

118. How do senior leaders deploy your organizations vision and values through your leadership system, to the workforce, to key suppliers and partners, and to customers and other stakeholders, as appropriate?
<--- Score

119. If you were responsible for initiating and implementing major changes in your organization, what steps might you take to ensure acceptance of those changes?
<--- Score

120. Is a Applied behavior analysis team work effort in place?
<--- Score

121. What business benefits will Applied behavior analysis goals deliver if achieved?
<--- Score

122. If you had to rebuild your organization without any traditional competitive advantages (i.e., no killer technology, promising research, innovative product/service delivery model, etcetera), how would your people have to approach their work and collaborate together in order to create the necessary conditions for success?
<--- Score

123. Who are four people whose careers you have enhanced?

<--- Score

124. Why is Applied behavior analysis important for you now?

<--- Score

125. How will you know that the Applied behavior analysis project has been successful?

<--- Score

126. How do you govern and fulfill your societal responsibilities?

<--- Score

127. Do you see more potential in people than they do in themselves?

<--- Score

128. How do you go about securing Applied behavior analysis?

<--- Score

129. What happens when a new employee joins the organization?

<--- Score

130. What potential megatrends could make your business model obsolete?

<--- Score

131. Operational - will it work?

<--- Score

132. Can you maintain your growth without

detracting from the factors that have contributed to your success?
<--- Score

133. Are you / should you be revolutionary or evolutionary?
<--- Score

134. Who are the key stakeholders?
<--- Score

135. What one word do you want to own in the minds of your customers, employees, and partners?
<--- Score

136. Is Applied behavior analysis realistic, or are you setting yourself up for failure?
<--- Score

137. Do you know who is a friend or a foe?
<--- Score

138. What stupid rule would you most like to kill?
<--- Score

139. Were lessons learned captured and communicated?
<--- Score

140. In the past year, what have you done (or could you have done) to increase the accurate perception of your company/brand as ethical and honest?
<--- Score

141. How are you doing compared to your industry?
<--- Score

142. What is the big Applied behavior analysis idea?
<--- Score

143. Who is responsible for Applied behavior analysis?
<--- Score

144. If no one would ever find out about your accomplishments, how would you lead differently?
<--- Score

145. Do you feel that more should be done in the Applied behavior analysis area?
<--- Score

146. What is the recommended frequency of auditing?
<--- Score

147. How can you negotiate Applied behavior analysis successfully with a stubborn boss, an irate client, or a deceitful coworker?
<--- Score

148. If you got fired and a new hire took your place, what would she do different?
<--- Score

149. Do you have an implicit bias for capital investments over people investments?
<--- Score

150. How do you manage Applied behavior analysis Knowledge Management (KM)?
<--- Score

151. Whom among your colleagues do you trust, and

for what?
<--- Score

152. Is there any reason to believe the opposite of my current belief?
<--- Score

153. What have you done to protect your business from competitive encroachment?
<--- Score

154. To whom do you add value?
<--- Score

155. What is the kind of project structure that would be appropriate for your Applied behavior analysis project, should it be formal and complex, or can it be less formal and relatively simple?
<--- Score

156. Who have you, as a company, historically been when you've been at your best?
<--- Score

157. What are the long-term Applied behavior analysis goals?
<--- Score

158. How do you set Applied behavior analysis stretch targets and how do you get people to not only participate in setting these stretch targets but also that they strive to achieve these?
<--- Score

159. What knowledge, skills and characteristics mark a good Applied behavior analysis project manager?

<--- Score

160. What you are going to do to affect the numbers?
<--- Score

161. Who, on the executive team or the board, has spoken to a customer recently?
<--- Score

162. What are your personal philosophies regarding Applied behavior analysis and how do they influence your work?
<--- Score

163. What happens if you do not have enough funding?
<--- Score

164. Which Applied behavior analysis goals are the most important?
<--- Score

165. How likely is it that a customer would recommend your company to a friend or colleague?
<--- Score

166. How do you assess the Applied behavior analysis pitfalls that are inherent in implementing it?
<--- Score

167. Are all key stakeholders present at all Structured Walkthroughs?
<--- Score

168. How do you proactively clarify deliverables and Applied behavior analysis quality expectations?

<--- Score

169. If you had to leave your organization for a year and the only communication you could have with employees/colleagues was a single paragraph, what would you write?
<--- Score

170. Is your basic point _____ or _____?
<--- Score

171. How important is Applied behavior analysis to the user organizations mission?
<--- Score

172. What is the purpose of Applied behavior analysis in relation to the mission?
<--- Score

173. Ask yourself: how would you do this work if you only had one staff member to do it?
<--- Score

174. In retrospect, of the projects that you pulled the plug on, what percent do you wish had been allowed to keep going, and what percent do you wish had ended earlier?
<--- Score

175. Do you have enough freaky customers in your portfolio pushing you to the limit day in and day out?
<--- Score

176. Have new benefits been realized?
<--- Score

177. Do you think you know, or do you know you know ?
<--- Score

178. How will you ensure you get what you expected?
<--- Score

179. What are the potential basics of Applied behavior analysis fraud?
<--- Score

180. Are new benefits received and understood?
<--- Score

181. Is Applied behavior analysis dependent on the successful delivery of a current project?
<--- Score

182. Who will provide the final approval of Applied behavior analysis deliverables?
<--- Score

183. If there were zero limitations, what would you do differently?
<--- Score

184. How can you become more high-tech but still be high touch?
<--- Score

185. What is the overall business strategy?
<--- Score

186. What are the success criteria that will indicate that Applied behavior analysis objectives have been met and the benefits delivered?

<--- Score

187. What role does communication play in the success or failure of a Applied behavior analysis project?
<--- Score

188. Is a Applied behavior analysis breakthrough on the horizon?
<--- Score

189. Are you relevant? Will you be relevant five years from now? Ten?
<--- Score

190. What are the rules and assumptions your industry operates under? What if the opposite were true?
<--- Score

191. What are current Applied behavior analysis paradigms?
<--- Score

192. Is the impact that Applied behavior analysis has shown?
<--- Score

193. How do you keep records, of what?
<--- Score

194. Why do and why don't your customers like your organization?
<--- Score

195. Why should people listen to you?
<--- Score

196. How much does Applied behavior analysis help?
<--- Score

197. What did you miss in the interview for the worst hire you ever made?
<--- Score

198. What could happen if you do not do it?
<--- Score

199. How do you foster innovation?
<--- Score

200. What is your BATNA (best alternative to a negotiated agreement)?
<--- Score

201. How do you deal with Applied behavior analysis changes?
<--- Score

202. Who else should you help?
<--- Score

203. Why should you adopt a Applied behavior analysis framework?
<--- Score

204. What relationships among Applied behavior analysis trends do you perceive?
<--- Score

205. Are you satisfied with your current role? If not, what is missing from it?
<--- Score

206. Can the schedule be done in the given time?
<--- Score

207. If your company went out of business tomorrow, would anyone who doesn't get a paycheck here care?
<--- Score

208. What is a feasible sequencing of reform initiatives over time?
<--- Score

209. If you find that you havent accomplished one of the goals for one of the steps of the Applied behavior analysis strategy, what will you do to fix it?
<--- Score

210. Where do you find information on writing acceptable supervision goals?
<--- Score

211. Do you have the right capabilities and capacities?
<--- Score

212. How do you transition from the baseline to the target?
<--- Score

213. What is the overall talent health of your organization as a whole at senior levels, and for each organization reporting to a member of the Senior Leadership Team?
<--- Score

Add up total points for this section:
_____ = Total points for this section

Divided by: _____ (number of statements answered) = _____
Average score for this section

Transfer your score to the Applied behavior analysis Index at the beginning of the Self-Assessment.

Applied behavior analysis and Managing Projects, Criteria for Project Managers:

1.0 Initiating Process Group: Applied behavior analysis

1. How will you do it?

2. Do you know the Applied behavior analysis projects goal, purpose and objectives?

3. What is the stake of others in your Applied behavior analysis project?

4. Do you understand all business (operational), technical, resource and vendor risks associated with the Applied behavior analysis project?

5. At which stage, in a typical Applied behavior analysis project do stake holders have maximum influence?

6. What communication items need improvement?

7. What are the constraints?

8. What do you need to do?

9. Were sponsors and decision makers available when needed outside regularly scheduled meetings?

10. What do they need to know about the Applied behavior analysis project?

11. Just how important is your work to the overall success of the Applied behavior analysis project?

12. Realistic - are the desired results expressed in a

way that the team will be motivated and believe that the required level of involvement will be obtained?

13. What will be the pressing issues of tomorrow?

14. Based on your Applied behavior analysis project communication management plan, what worked well?

15. What are the tools and techniques to be used in each phase?

16. Were decisions made in a timely manner?

17. What were the challenges that you encountered during the execution of a previous Applied behavior analysis project that you would not want to repeat?

18. Are the changes in your Applied behavior analysis project being formally requested, analyzed, and approved by the appropriate decision makers?

19. Are you just doing busywork to pass the time?

20. Have the stakeholders identified all individual requirements pertaining to business process?

1.1 Project Charter: Applied behavior analysis

21. Why the improvements?

22. When is a charter needed?

23. Where and how does the team fit within your organization structure?

24. What changes can you make to improve?

25. Are you building in-house ?

26. When will this occur?

27. Applied behavior analysis project deliverables: what is the Applied behavior analysis project going to produce?

28. Market – identify products market, including whether it is outside of the objective: what is the purpose of the program or Applied behavior analysis project?

29. When do you use a Applied behavior analysis project Charter?

30. What material?

31. Who is the sponsor?

32. How do you manage integration?

33. Success determination factors: how will the success of the Applied behavior analysis project be determined from the customers perspective?

34. Applied behavior analysis project background: what is the primary motivation for this Applied behavior analysis project?

35. What ideas do you have for initial tests of change (PDSA cycles)?

36. Must Have?

37. Are there special technology requirements?

38. Fit with other Products Compliments – Cannibalizes?

39. How much?

40. What goes into your Applied behavior analysis project Charter?

1.2 Stakeholder Register: Applied behavior analysis

41. Who wants to talk about Security?

42. What are the major Applied behavior analysis project milestones requiring communications or providing communications opportunities?

43. What & Why?

44. Who is managing stakeholder engagement?

45. Who are the stakeholders?

46. How big is the gap?

47. Is your organization ready for change?

48. What is the power of the stakeholder?

49. What opportunities exist to provide communications?

50. How much influence do they have on the Applied behavior analysis project?

51. How should employers make voices heard?

52. How will reports be created?

1.3 Stakeholder Analysis Matrix: Applied behavior analysis

53. Cashflow, start-up cash-drain?

54. Lack of competitive strength?

55. Vulnerable groups; who are the vulnerable groups that might be affected by the Applied behavior analysis project?

56. Volumes, production, economies?

57. What do people from other organizations see as your organizations weaknesses?

58. Who holds positions of responsibility in interested organizations?

59. How does the Applied behavior analysis project involve consultations or collaboration with other organizations?

60. Who is most interested in information about the topic and/or has previously initiated interest?

61. Processes, systems, it, communications?

62. What do you Evaluate?

63. Is changing technology threatening your organizations position?

64. Why do you care?

65. Insurmountable weaknesses?

66. Who will promote/support the Applied behavior analysis project, provided that they are involved?

67. Participatory approach: how will key stakeholders participate in the Applied behavior analysis project?

68. Sustainable financial backing?

69. How affected by the problem(s)?

70. What tools would help you communicate?

71. Who is influential in the Applied behavior analysis project area (both thematic and geographic areas)?

72. Supporters; who are the supporters?

2.0 Planning Process Group: Applied behavior analysis

73. If a task is partitionable, is this a sufficient condition to reduce the Applied behavior analysis project duration?

74. Have more efficient (sensitive) and appropriate measures been adopted to respond to the political and socio-cultural problems identified?

75. In which Applied behavior analysis project management process group is the detailed Applied behavior analysis project budget created?

76. When developing the estimates for Applied behavior analysis project phases, you choose to add the individual estimates for the activities that comprise each phase. What type of estimation method are you using?

77. What is the critical path for this Applied behavior analysis project, and what is the duration of the critical path?

78. Does it make any difference if you are successful?

79. To what extent do the intervention objectives and strategies of the Applied behavior analysis project respond to your organizations plans?

80. If you are late, will anybody notice?

81. To what extent has a PMO contributed to raising the quality of the design of the Applied behavior analysis project?

82. How well do the team follow the chosen processes?

83. Are work methodologies, financial instruments, etc. shared among departments, organizations and Applied behavior analysis projects?

84. On which process should team members spend the most time?

85. The Applied behavior analysis project charter is created in which Applied behavior analysis project management process group?

86. What good practices or successful experiences or transferable examples have been identified?

87. How does activity resource estimation affect activity duration estimation?

88. How will you know you did it?

89. First of all, should any action be taken?

90. How can you tell when you are done?

91. How many days can task X be late in starting without affecting the Applied behavior analysis project completion date?

92. Is the Applied behavior analysis project supported by national and/or local organizations?

2.1 Project Management Plan: Applied behavior analysis

93. Who manages integration?

94. Is the budget realistic?

95. Is mitigation authorized or recommended?

96. What are the assigned resources?

97. How do you manage time?

98. Do there need to be organizational changes?

99. Are there any client staffing expectations?

100. Is the engineering content at a feasibility level-of-detail, and is it sufficiently complete, to provide an adequate basis for the baseline cost estimate?

101. What would you do differently?

102. What does management expect of PMs?

103. How can you best help your organization to develop consistent practices in Applied behavior analysis project management planning stages?

104. What is the business need?

105. Has the selected plan been formulated using cost effectiveness and incremental analysis techniques?

106. Was the peer (technical) review of the cost estimates duly coordinated with the cost estimate center of expertise and addressed in the review documentation and certification?

107. Are alternatives safe, functional, constructible, economical, reasonable and sustainable?

2.2 Scope Management Plan: Applied behavior analysis

108. What are the Quality Assurance overheads?

109. Which statement about customer expectations is not true?

110. Do all stakeholders know how to access this repository and where to find the Applied behavior analysis project documentation?

111. Has your organization readiness assessment been conducted?

112. Have adequate resources been provided by management to ensure Applied behavior analysis project success?

113. Are there procedures in place to effectively manage interdependencies with other Applied behavior analysis projects, systems, Vendors and your organizations work effort?

114. Why is a scope management plan important?

115. Have the procedures for identifying budget variances been followed?

116. Is there an on-going process in place to monitor Applied behavior analysis project risks?

117. Is the communication plan being followed?

118. What is the most common tool for helping define the detail?

119. Is current scope of the Applied behavior analysis project substantially different than that originally defined?

120. Are the appropriate IT resources adequate to meet planned commitments?

121. Is the schedule updated on a periodic basis?

122. Are adequate resources provided for the quality assurance function?

123. Are the budget estimates reasonable?

124. Are risk oriented checklists used during risk identification?

125. Do you have funding for Applied behavior analysis project and product development, implementation and on-going support?

126. Has the budget been baselined?

127. Has a resource management plan been created?

2.3 Requirements Management Plan: Applied behavior analysis

128. In case of software development; Should you have a test for each code module?

129. Is the system software (non-operating system) new to the IT Applied behavior analysis project team?

130. Who will perform the analysis?

131. Business analysis scope?

132. Is it new or replacing an existing business system or process?

133. Did you provide clear and concise specifications?

134. Is the user satisfied?

135. How will you develop the schedule of requirements activities?

136. How will the information be distributed?

137. Will you perform a Requirements Risk assessment and develop a plan to deal with risks?

138. Describe the process for rejecting the Applied behavior analysis project requirements. Who has the authority to reject Applied behavior analysis project requirements?

139. Are actual resources expenditures versus planned expenditures acceptable?

140. Do you have price sheets and a methodology for determining the total proposal cost?

141. Are actual resource expenditures versus planned still acceptable?

142. What are you counting on?

143. How will bidders price evaluations be done, by deliverables, phases, or in a big bang?

144. Who will finally present the work or product(s) for acceptance?

145. Is any organizational data being used or stored?

146. If it exists, where is it housed?

147. What went right?

2.4 Requirements Documentation: Applied behavior analysis

148. How do you know when a Requirement is accurate enough?

149. What can tools do for us?

150. Who is involved?

151. How does what is being described meet the business need?

152. What images does it conjure?

153. What is your Elevator Speech?

154. Is new technology needed?

155. How much does requirements engineering cost?

156. How to document system requirements?

157. Do your constraints stand?

158. How can you document system requirements?

159. Basic work/business process; high-level, what is being touched?

160. What is a show stopper in the requirements?

161. Are there legal issues?

162. How will they be documented / shared?

163. Does your organization restrict technical alternatives?

164. What are the acceptance criteria?

165. What happens when requirements are wrong?

166. Validity. does the system provide the functions which best support the customers needs?

167. How will requirements be documented and who signs off on them?

2.5 Requirements Traceability Matrix: Applied behavior analysis

168. Will you use a Requirements Traceability Matrix?

169. Why do you manage scope?

170. What is the WBS?

171. Describe the process for approving requirements so they can be added to the traceability matrix and Applied behavior analysis project work can be performed. Will the Applied behavior analysis project requirements become approved in writing?

172. How will it affect the stakeholders personally in career?

173. How do you manage scope?

174. Why use a WBS?

175. Do you have a clear understanding of all subcontracts in place?

176. How small is small enough?

177. What percentage of Applied behavior analysis projects are producing traceability matrices between requirements and other work products?

178. Is there a requirements traceability process in place?

179. What are the chronologies, contingencies, consequences, criteria?

2.6 Project Scope Statement: Applied behavior analysis

180. Is this process communicated to the customer and team members?

181. Were potential customers involved early in the planning process?

182. Are the meetings set up to have assigned note takers that will add action/issues to the issue list?

183. Did your Applied behavior analysis project ask for this?

184. Are there backup strategies for key members of the Applied behavior analysis project?

185. Are there completion/verification criteria defined for each task producing an output?

186. Is an issue management process documented and filed?

187. Will all Applied behavior analysis project issues be unconditionally tracked through the issue resolution process?

188. Write a brief purpose statement for this Applied behavior analysis project. Include a business justification statement. What is the product of this Applied behavior analysis project?

189. How will you verify the accuracy of the work of the Applied behavior analysis project, and what constitutes acceptance of the deliverables?

190. Is the Applied behavior analysis project manager qualified and experienced in Applied behavior analysis project management?

191. Has the format for tracking and monitoring schedules and costs been defined?

192. Any new risks introduced or old risks impacted. Are there issues that could affect the existing requirements for the result, service, or product if the scope changes?

193. Are there issues that could affect the existing requirements for the result, service, or product if the scope changes?

194. If there are vendors, have they signed off on the Applied behavior analysis project Plan?

195. Why do you need to manage scope?

196. Is there a Quality Assurance Plan documented and filed?

197. Will statistics related to QA be collected, trends analyzed, and problems raised as issues?

2.7 Assumption and Constraint Log: Applied behavior analysis

198. Model-building: what data-analytic strategies are useful when building proportional-hazards models?

199. How are new requirements or changes to requirements identified?

200. Are funding and staffing resource estimates sufficiently detailed and documented for use in planning and tracking the Applied behavior analysis project?

201. What to do at recovery?

202. What do you audit?

203. Have all involved stakeholders and work groups committed to the Applied behavior analysis project?

204. Have all stakeholders been identified?

205. Has the approach and development strategy of the Applied behavior analysis project been defined, documented and accepted by the appropriate stakeholders?

206. Contradictory information between different documents?

207. Is the process working, and people are not executing in compliance of the process?

208. How can constraints be violated?

209. Has a Applied behavior analysis project Communications Plan been developed?

210. How do you design an auditing system?

211. Is this process still needed?

212. Is the definition of the Applied behavior analysis project scope clear; what needs to be accomplished?

213. Does the document/deliverable meet general requirements (for example, statement of work) for all deliverables?

214. Is there documentation of system capability requirements, data requirements, environment requirements, security requirements, and computer and hardware requirements?

215. Are there processes in place to ensure that all the terms and code concepts have been documented consistently?

216. What weaknesses do you have?

217. Does the system design reflect the requirements?

2.8 Work Breakdown Structure: Applied behavior analysis

218. Where does it take place?

219. Is it a change in scope?

220. How far down?

221. How much detail?

222. Is it still viable?

223. Why is it useful?

224. Is the work breakdown structure (wbs) defined and is the scope of the Applied behavior analysis project clear with assigned deliverable owners?

225. When does it have to be done?

226. What is the probability that the Applied behavior analysis project duration will exceed xx weeks?

227. What has to be done?

228. When do you stop?

229. Who has to do it?

230. When would you develop a Work Breakdown Structure?

231. Can you make it?

232. Do you need another level?

233. How big is a work-package?

2.9 WBS Dictionary: Applied behavior analysis

234. Does the contractors system provide for determination of price variance by comparing planned Vs actual commitments?

235. Is each control account assigned to a single organizational element directly responsible for the work and identifiable to a single element of the CWBS?

236. Are management actions taken to reduce indirect costs when there are significant adverse variances?

237. Is undistributed budget limited to contract effort which cannot yet be planned to CWBS elements at or below the level specified for reporting to the Government?

238. Are the bases and rates for allocating costs from each indirect pool to commercial work consistent with the already stated used to allocate corresponding costs to Government contracts?

239. Is the entire contract planned in time-phased control accounts to the extent practicable?

240. Intermediate schedules, as required, which provide a logical sequence from the master schedule to the control account level?

241. Are retroactive changes to BCWS and BCWP prohibited except for correction of errors or for normal accounting adjustments?

242. What went wrong?

243. Are the procedures for identifying indirect costs to incurring organizations, indirect cost pools, and allocating the costs from the pools to the contracts formally documented?

244. Are internal budgets for authorized, and not priced changes based on the contractors resource plan for accomplishing the work?

245. Changes in the nature of the overhead requirements?

246. Are records maintained to show how management reserves are used?

247. Do work packages reflect the actual way in which the work will be done and are they meaningful products or management-oriented subdivisions of a higher level element of work?

248. Does the scheduling system provide for the identification of work progress against technical and other milestones, and also provide for forecasts of completion dates of scheduled work?

249. Evaluate the performance of operating organizations?

250. The wbs is developed as part of a joint planning session. and how do you know that youhave done this

right?

251. The anticipated business volume?

252. Are data elements reconcilable between internal summary reports and reports forwarded to us?

2.10 Schedule Management Plan: Applied behavior analysis

253. Is a process defined to measure the performance of the schedule management process itself?

254. Who is responsible for estimating the activity resources?

255. Must the Applied behavior analysis project be complete by a specified date?

256. Has the Applied behavior analysis project scope been baselined?

257. Alignment to strategic goals & objectives?

258. List all schedule constraints here. Must the Applied behavior analysis project be complete by a specified date?

259. Are changes in scope (deliverable commitments) agreed to by all affected groups & individuals?

260. Are all resource assumptions documented?

261. Are the people assigned to the Applied behavior analysis project sufficiently qualified?

262. Why conduct schedule analysis?

263. Is the development plan and/or process documented?

264. Has the schedule been baselined?

265. What will be the format of the schedule model?

266. Does the Applied behavior analysis project have a Statement of Work?

267. Have the key elements of a coherent Applied behavior analysis project management strategy been established?

268. What is the difference between % Complete and % work?

269. Has a capability assessment been conducted?

270. Are all activities logically sequenced?

2.11 Activity List: Applied behavior analysis

271. Can you determine the activity that must finish, before this activity can start?

272. What is the total time required to complete the Applied behavior analysis project if no delays occur?

273. How do you determine the late start (LS) for each activity?

274. In what sequence?

275. Should you include sub-activities?

276. When will the work be performed?

277. What is your organizations history in doing similar activities?

278. Who will perform the work?

279. When do the individual activities need to start and finish?

280. What is the LF and LS for each activity?

281. For other activities, how much delay can be tolerated?

282. What went well?

283. Is there anything planned that does not need to be here?

284. What did not go as well?

285. Are the required resources available or need to be acquired?

286. What will be performed?

2.12 Activity Attributes: Applied behavior analysis

287. Do you feel very comfortable with your prediction?

288. How many resources do you need to complete the work scope within a limit of X number of days?

289. Were there other ways you could have organized the data to achieve similar results?

290. Does your organization of the data change its meaning?

291. How difficult will it be to do specific activities on this Applied behavior analysis project?

292. Resources to accomplish the work?

293. How difficult will it be to complete specific activities on this Applied behavior analysis project?

294. What conclusions/generalizations can you draw from this?

295. What is missing?

296. How much activity detail is required?

297. What activity do you think you should spend the most time on?

298. How else could the items be grouped?

299. Can you re-assign any activities to another resource to resolve an over-allocation?

300. Are the required resources available?

301. Activity: what is Missing?

302. Where else does it apply?

303. Have you identified the Activity Leveling Priority code value on each activity?

2.13 Milestone List: Applied behavior analysis

304. How soon can the activity finish?

305. It is to be a narrative text providing the crucial aspects of your Applied behavior analysis project proposal answering what, who, how, when and where?

306. How soon can the activity start?

307. Environmental effects?

308. What would happen if a delivery of material was one week late?

309. Usps (unique selling points)?

310. When will the Applied behavior analysis project be complete?

311. New USPs?

312. Which path is the critical path?

313. How will the milestone be verified?

314. Gaps in capabilities?

315. Reliability of data, plan predictability?

316. How late can the activity start?

317. How late can the activity finish?

318. Calculate how long can activity be delayed?

2.14 Network Diagram: Applied behavior analysis

319. Where do schedules come from?

320. What must be completed before an activity can be started?

321. Exercise: what is the probability that the Applied behavior analysis project duration will exceed xx weeks?

322. Are you on time?

323. Are the gantt chart and/or network diagram updated periodically and used to assess the overall Applied behavior analysis project timetable?

324. What activities must follow this activity?

325. What are the tools?

326. Which type of network diagram allows you to depict four types of dependencies?

327. If the Applied behavior analysis project network diagram cannot change and you have extra personnel resources, what is the BEST thing to do?

328. Why must you schedule milestones, such as reviews, throughout the Applied behavior analysis project?

329. Where do you schedule uncertainty time?

330. How confident can you be in your milestone dates and the delivery date?

331. What activities must occur simultaneously with this activity?

332. If x is long, what would be the completion time if you break x into two parallel parts of y weeks and z weeks?

333. What activity must be completed immediately before this activity can start?

334. How difficult will it be to do specific activities on this Applied behavior analysis project?

335. What is the lowest cost to complete this Applied behavior analysis project in xx weeks?

336. What to do and When?

337. If a current contract exists, can you provide the vendor name, contract start, and contract expiration date?

2.15 Activity Resource Requirements: Applied behavior analysis

338. Which logical relationship does the PDM use most often?

339. What are constraints that you might find during the Human Resource Planning process?

340. When does monitoring begin?

341. How many signatures do you require on a check and does this match what is in your policy and procedures?

342. Time for overtime?

343. How do you handle petty cash?

344. Are there unresolved issues that need to be addressed?

345. Organizational Applicability?

346. Why do you do that?

347. What is the Work Plan Standard?

348. Do you use tools like decomposition and rolling-wave planning to produce the activity list and other outputs?

349. Other support in specific areas?

350. Anything else?

2.16 Resource Breakdown Structure: Applied behavior analysis

351. Who is allowed to see what data about which resources?

352. How can this help you with team building?

353. What can you do to improve productivity?

354. The list could probably go on, but, the thing that you would most like to know is, How long & How much?

355. How difficult will it be to do specific activities on this Applied behavior analysis project?

356. Which resources should be in the resource pool?

357. Why time management?

358. When do they need the information?

359. Who is allowed to perform which functions?

360. What defines a successful Applied behavior analysis project?

361. Who needs what information?

362. Why is this important?

363. Why do you do it?

364. Who will be used as a Applied behavior analysis project team member?

2.17 Activity Duration Estimates: Applied behavior analysis

365. Explanation notice how many choices are half right?

366. After changes are approved are Applied behavior analysis project documents updated and distributed?

367. Will it help in finding or retaining employees?

368. Does the case present a realistic scenario?

369. Are expert judgment and historical information utilized to estimate activity duration?

370. Are reward and recognition systems defined to promote or reinforce desired behavior?

371. Are procedures defined for calculating cost estimates?

372. What is the critical path for this Applied behavior analysis project and how long is it?

373. Are Applied behavior analysis project activities decomposed into manageable components to ensure expected management control?

374. Why is it difficult to use Applied behavior analysis project management software well?

375. What is earned value?

376. What are the Applied behavior analysis project management deliverables of each process group?

377. Account for the make-or-buy process and how to perform the financial calculations involved in the process. What are the main types of contracts if you do decide to outsource?

378. Are tools and techniques defined for gathering, integrating and distributing Applied behavior analysis project outputs?

379. Does a process exist to identify which qualified resources may be attainable?

380. What should be done NEXT?

381. Which skills do you think are most important for an information technology Applied behavior analysis project manager?

382. Does a process exist to determine which risk events to accept and which events to disregard?

383. How can others help Applied behavior analysis project managers understand your organizational context for Applied behavior analysis projects?

2.18 Duration Estimating Worksheet: Applied behavior analysis

384. Can the Applied behavior analysis project be constructed as planned?

385. How can the Applied behavior analysis project be displayed graphically to better visualize the activities?

386. What are the critical bottleneck activities?

387. When, then?

388. What is next?

389. Why estimate time and cost?

390. What utility impacts are there?

391. What info is needed?

392. Science = process: remember the scientific method?

393. What is an Average Applied behavior analysis project?

394. What is the total time required to complete the Applied behavior analysis project if no delays occur?

395. How should ongoing costs be monitored to try to keep the Applied behavior analysis project within budget?

396. What work will be included in the Applied behavior analysis project?

397. What is your role?

398. What is cost and Applied behavior analysis project cost management?

399. When does your organization expect to be able to complete it?

400. Is a construction detail attached (to aid in explanation)?

2.19 Project Schedule: Applied behavior analysis

401. Does the condition or event threaten the Applied behavior analysis projects objectives in any ways?

402. How can you address that situation?

403. Why do you need to manage Applied behavior analysis project Risk?

404. Are the original Applied behavior analysis project schedule and budget realistic?

405. Is Applied behavior analysis project work proceeding in accordance with the original Applied behavior analysis project schedule?

406. How closely did the initial Applied behavior analysis project Schedule compare with the actual schedule?

407. Is infrastructure setup part of your Applied behavior analysis project?

408. Meet requirements?

409. How do you manage Applied behavior analysis project Risk?

410. Your Applied behavior analysis project management plan results in a Applied behavior analysis project schedule that is too long. If the

Applied behavior analysis project network diagram cannot change and you have extra personnel resources, what is the BEST thing to do?

411. Eliminate unnecessary activities. Are there activities that came from a template or previous Applied behavior analysis project that are not applicable on this phase of this Applied behavior analysis project?

412. Is there a Schedule Management Plan that establishes the criteria and activities for developing, monitoring and controlling the Applied behavior analysis project schedule?

413. Are quality inspections and review activities listed in the Applied behavior analysis project schedule(s)?

414. To what degree is do you feel the entire team was committed to the Applied behavior analysis project schedule?

415. Are all remaining durations correct?

416. What is the most mis-scheduled part of process?

417. How does a Applied behavior analysis project get to be a year late ?

418. Are procedures defined by which the Applied behavior analysis project schedule may be changed?

419. How detailed should a Applied behavior analysis project get?

2.20 Cost Management Plan: Applied behavior analysis

420. Will the earned value reporting interface between time and cost management?

421. Have all unresolved risks been documented?

422. What would you do differently what did not work?

423. Has a sponsor been identified?

424. Are the results of quality assurance reviews provided to affected groups & individuals?

425. Is your organization certified as a supplier, wholesaler and/or regular dealer?

426. Are enough systems & user personnel assigned to the Applied behavior analysis project?

427. Are target dates established for each milestone deliverable?

428. Are vendor contract reports, reviews and visits conducted periodically?

429. Are key risk mitigation strategies added to the Applied behavior analysis project schedule?

430. If you sold 10x widgets on a day, what would the affect on costs be?

431. Has a Applied behavior analysis project Communications Plan been developed?

432. Is the steering committee active in Applied behavior analysis project oversight?

433. Cost / benefit analysis?

434. What strengths do you have?

435. Is there a requirements change management processes in place?

436. Are metrics used to evaluate and manage Vendors?

437. Is there an issues management plan in place?

438. Are all payments made according to the contract(s)?

439. Is it possible to track all classes of Applied behavior analysis project work (e.g. scheduled, unscheduled, defect repair, etc.)?

2.21 Activity Cost Estimates: Applied behavior analysis

440. Vac -variance at completion, how much over/under budget do you expect to be?

441. What areas does the group agree are the biggest success on the Applied behavior analysis project?

442. What were things that you did well, and could improve, and how?

443. What is a Applied behavior analysis project Management Plan?

444. What is the activity inventory?

445. How do you change activities?

446. Is there anything unique in this Applied behavior analysis projects scope statement that will affect resources?

447. Why do you manage cost?

448. How do you allocate indirect costs to activities?

449. What do you want to know about the stay to know if costs were inappropriately high or low?

450. How many activities should you have?

451. Did the consultant work with local staff to

develop local capacity?

452. What is the Applied behavior analysis projects sustainability strategy that will ensure Applied behavior analysis project results will endure or be sustained?

453. If you are asked to lower your estimate because the price is too high, what are your options?

454. Based on your Applied behavior analysis project communication management plan, what worked well?

455. What skill level is required to do the job?

456. Were the tasks or work products prepared by the consultant useful?

457. What is the activity recast of the budget?

458. What are you looking for?

2.22 Cost Estimating Worksheet: Applied behavior analysis

459. What happens to any remaining funds not used?

460. Value pocket identification & quantification what are value pockets?

461. What can be included?

462. What additional Applied behavior analysis project(s) could be initiated as a result of this Applied behavior analysis project?

463. Is the Applied behavior analysis project responsive to community need?

464. What costs are to be estimated?

465. Will the Applied behavior analysis project collaborate with the local community and leverage resources?

466. Does the Applied behavior analysis project provide innovative ways for stakeholders to overcome obstacles or deliver better outcomes?

467. Identify the timeframe necessary to monitor progress and collect data to determine how the selected measure has changed?

468. Can a trend be established from historical performance data on the selected measure and are

the criteria for using trend analysis or forecasting methods met?

469. What is the estimated labor cost today based upon this information?

470. What will others want?

471. How will the results be shared and to whom?

472. What is the purpose of estimating?

473. Ask: are others positioned to know, are others credible, and will others cooperate?

474. Who is best positioned to know and assist in identifying corresponding factors?

475. Is it feasible to establish a control group arrangement?

2.23 Cost Baseline: Applied behavior analysis

476. Impact to environment?

477. Have the resources used by the Applied behavior analysis project been reassigned to other units or Applied behavior analysis projects?

478. How fast?

479. How will cost estimates be used?

480. Are you asking management for something as a result of this update?

481. When should cost estimates be developed?

482. Are you meeting with your team regularly?

483. What threats might prevent you from getting there?

484. Has the documentation relating to operation and maintenance of the product(s) or service(s) been delivered to, and accepted by, operations management?

485. What deliverables come first?

486. Has training and knowledge transfer of the operations organization been completed?

487. What is the most important thing to do next to make your Applied behavior analysis project successful?

488. On time?

489. How likely is it to go wrong?

490. Review your risk triggers -have your risks changed?

2.24 Quality Management Plan: Applied behavior analysis

491. Are there ways to reduce the time it takes to get something approved?

492. How are data handled when a test is not run per specification?

493. How will you know that a change is actually an improvement?

494. Is there a procedure for this process?

495. What data do you gather/use/compile?

496. If it is out of compliance, should the process be amended or should the Plan be amended?

497. What has the QM Collaboration done?

498. Does a documented Applied behavior analysis project organizational policy & plan (i.e. governance model) exist?

499. Have all involved stakeholders and work groups committed to the Applied behavior analysis project?

500. Who is approving the QAPP?

501. How do you ensure that protocols are up to date?

502. How are people conducting sampling trained?

503. Has a Applied behavior analysis project Communications Plan been developed?

504. Does the program conduct field testing?

505. Results Available?

506. What are your organizations current levels and trends for the already stated measures related to customer satisfaction/ dissatisfaction and product/ service performance?

507. Are there nonconformance issues?

508. What are you trying to accomplish?

509. Diagrams and tables to account for complex concepts and increase overall readability?

2.25 Quality Metrics: Applied behavior analysis

510. What forces exist that would cause them to change?

511. What does this tell us?

512. Are quality metrics defined?

513. How is it being measured?

514. Should a modifier be included?

515. There are many reasons to shore up quality-related metrics, and what metrics are important?

516. How do you know if everyone is trying to improve the right things?

517. Are applicable standards referenced and available?

518. What happens if you get an abnormal result?

519. Has risk analysis been adequately reviewed?

520. Were quality attributes reported?

521. What makes a visualization memorable?

522. Which are the right metrics to use?

523. What is the benchmark?

524. What if the biggest risk to your business were the already stated people who do not complain?

525. What method of measurement do you use?

526. Where is quality now?

527. Subjective quality component: customer satisfaction, how do you measure it?

528. What level of statistical confidence do you use?

2.26 Process Improvement Plan: Applied behavior analysis

529. What is the return on investment?

530. What personnel are the change agents for your initiative?

531. To elicit goal statements, do you ask a question such as, What do you want to achieve?

532. Purpose of goal: the motive is determined by asking, why do you want to achieve this goal?

533. What lessons have you learned so far?

534. What is quality and how will you ensure it?

535. Are you making progress on the improvement framework?

536. How do you manage quality?

537. Why quality management?

538. The motive is determined by asking, Why do you want to achieve this goal?

539. What makes people good SPI coaches?

540. Has the time line required to move measurement results from the points of collection to databases or users been established?

541. Why do you want to achieve the goal?

542. Are there forms and procedures to collect and record the data?

543. Are you making progress on the goals?

544. Have the supporting tools been developed or acquired?

545. Does your process ensure quality?

546. Are you making progress on your improvement plan?

547. Have storage and access mechanisms and procedures been determined?

548. Where are you now?

2.27 Responsibility Assignment Matrix: Applied behavior analysis

549. Not any rs, as, or cs: if an identified role is only informed, should others be eliminated from the matrix?

550. What will the work cost?

551. Do you need to convince people that its well worth the time and effort?

552. Is every signing-off responsibility and every communicating responsibility critically necessary?

553. Contract line items and end items?

554. Are all authorized tasks assigned to identified organizational elements?

555. Most people let you know when others re too busy, and are others really too busy?

556. Major functional areas of contract effort?

557. Identify potential or actual overruns and underruns?

558. What do you do when people do not respond?

559. Changes in the current direct and Applied behavior analysis projected base?

560. Is work progressively subdivided into detailed work packages as requirements are defined?

561. Evaluate the impact of schedule changes, work around, etc?

562. How cost benefit analysis?

563. With too many people labeled as doing the work, are there too many hands involved?

564. Are data elements reconcilable between internal summary reports and reports forwarded to stakeholders?

565. Are the actual costs used for variance analysis reconcilable with data from the accounting system?

566. Ideas for developing soft skills at your organization?

567. Does the contractors system provide unit or lot costs when applicable?

568. Where does all this information come from?

2.28 Roles and Responsibilities: Applied behavior analysis

569. What should you highlight for improvement?

570. Have you ever been a part of this team?

571. Once the responsibilities are defined for the Applied behavior analysis project, have the deliverables, roles and responsibilities been clearly communicated to every participant?

572. Is feedback clearly communicated and non-judgmental?

573. Is the data complete?

574. Are governance roles and responsibilities documented?

575. Are Applied behavior analysis project team roles and responsibilities identified and documented?

576. Was the expectation clearly communicated?

577. What is working well?

578. Do you take the time to clearly define roles and responsibilities on Applied behavior analysis project tasks?

579. What expectations were met?

580. Are the quality assurance functions and related roles and responsibilities clearly defined?

581. Be specific; avoid generalities. Thank you and great work alone are insufficient. What exactly do you appreciate and why?

582. Who: who is involved?

583. What should you do now to ensure that you are exceeding expectations and excelling in your current position?

584. What specific behaviors did you observe?

585. Who is responsible for implementation activities and where will the functions, roles and responsibilities be defined?

586. What are your major roles and responsibilities in the area of performance measurement and assessment?

2.29 Human Resource Management Plan: Applied behavior analysis

587. Is there an approved case?

588. Is a pmo (Applied behavior analysis project management office) in place and provide oversight to the Applied behavior analysis project?

589. Is there an on-going process in place to monitor Applied behavior analysis project risks?

590. Are vendor invoices audited for accuracy before payment?

591. Is there a Steering Committee in place?

592. What commitments have been made?

593. Are the Applied behavior analysis project team members located locally to the users/stakeholders?

594. Are Applied behavior analysis project team members committed fulltime?

595. Is it standard practice to formally commit stakeholders to the Applied behavior analysis project via agreements?

596. Staffing Requirements?

597. Are all key components of a Quality Assurance Plan present?

598. Are tasks tracked by hours?

599. Are meeting objectives identified for each meeting?

600. Are the key elements of a Applied behavior analysis project Charter present?

601. Have Applied behavior analysis project management standards and procedures been identified / established and documented?

602. Are updated Applied behavior analysis project time & resource estimates reasonable based on the current Applied behavior analysis project stage?

603. How are you going to ensure that you have a well motivated workforce?

604. Are the Applied behavior analysis project plans updated on a frequent basis?

605. Is it possible to track all classes of Applied behavior analysis project work (e.g. scheduled, un-scheduled, defect repair, etc.)?

2.30 Communications Management Plan: Applied behavior analysis

606. Do you have members of your team responsible for certain stakeholders?

607. Who is responsible?

608. Do you feel a register helps?

609. Which team member will work with each stakeholder?

610. Timing: when do the effects of the communication take place?

611. Will messages be directly related to the release strategy or phases of the Applied behavior analysis project?

612. How will the person responsible for executing the communication item be notified?

613. Which stakeholders can influence others?

614. Is there an important stakeholder who is actively opposed and will not receive messages?

615. Who to learn from?

616. What approaches to you feel are the best ones to use?

617. What is Applied behavior analysis project communications management?

618. Is the stakeholder role recognized by your organization?

619. Are there common objectives between the team and the stakeholder?

620. What data is going to be required?

621. Why do you manage communications?

622. Are others needed?

623. Who needs to know and how much?

624. How much time does it take to do it?

2.31 Risk Management Plan: Applied behavior analysis

625. Are testing tools available and suitable?

626. What things might go wrong?

627. Technology risk: is the Applied behavior analysis project technically feasible?

628. Havent software Applied behavior analysis projects been late before?

629. How will the Applied behavior analysis project know if your organizations risk response actions were effective?

630. Do you train all developers in the process?

631. Are there new risks that mitigation strategies might introduce?

632. Are team members trained in the use of the tools?

633. Are flexibility and reuse paramount?

634. What is the cost to the Applied behavior analysis project if it does occur?

635. Are the required plans included, such as nonstructural flood risk management plans?

636. Could others have been better mitigated?

637. Does the software engineering team have the right mix of skills?

638. What will drive change?

639. Who should be notified of the occurrence of each of the indicators?

640. Anticipated volatility of the requirements?

641. How is the audit profession changing?

642. Degree of confidence in estimated size estimate?

643. Are requirements fully understood by the software engineering team and customers?

2.32 Risk Register: Applied behavior analysis

644. How well are risks controlled?

645. What is a Risk?

646. What can be done about it?

647. People risk -are people with appropriate skills available to help complete the Applied behavior analysis project?

648. Having taken action, how did the responses effect change, and where is the Applied behavior analysis project now?

649. Risk categories: what are the main categories of risks that should be addressed on this Applied behavior analysis project?

650. How could corresponding Risk affect the Applied behavior analysis project in terms of cost and schedule?

651. What would the impact to the Applied behavior analysis project objectives be should the risk arise?

652. What action, if any, has been taken to respond to the risk?

653. Does the evidence highlight any areas to advance opportunities or foster good relations. If yes

what steps will be taken?

654. Risk probability and impact: how will the probabilities and impacts of risk items be assessed?

655. What could prevent you delivering on the strategic program objectives and what is being done to mitigate corresponding issues?

656. What evidence do you have to justify the likelihood score of the risk (audit, incident report, claim, complaints, inspection, internal review)?

657. What are the main aims, objectives of the policy, strategy, or service and the intended outcomes?

658. Financial risk -can your organization afford to undertake the Applied behavior analysis project?

659. Are there other alternative controls that could be implemented?

660. What may happen or not go according to plan?

661. Who is going to do it?

662. Preventative actions - planned actions to reduce the likelihood a risk will occur and/or reduce the seriousness should it occur. What should you do now?

663. What is your current and future risk profile?

2.33 Probability and Impact Assessment: Applied behavior analysis

664. Are Applied behavior analysis project requirements stable?

665. What are the risks involved in appointing external agencies to manage the Applied behavior analysis project?

666. Management -what contingency plans do you have if the risk becomes a reality?

667. Are the risk data timely and relevant?

668. Is a software Applied behavior analysis project management tool available?

669. Have you worked with the customer in the past?

670. Does the customer have a solid idea of what is required?

671. Is the customer willing to participate in reviews?

672. What are its business ethics?

673. Are enough people available?

674. Who has experience with this?

675. Is the customer willing to establish rapid

communication links with the developer?

676. How solid is the Applied behavior analysis projection of competitive reaction?

677. Does the software interface with new or unproven hardware or unproven vendor products?

678. What can you do to minimize the impact if it does?

679. Can you avoid altogether some things that might go wrong?

680. Are there alternative opinions/solutions/ processes you should explore?

681. How much risk do others need to take?

682. Can the Applied behavior analysis project proceed without assuming the risk?

2.34 Probability and Impact Matrix: Applied behavior analysis

683. What can you do about it?

684. The customer requests a change to the Applied behavior analysis project that would increase the Applied behavior analysis project risk. Which should you do before ass the others?

685. Has something like this been done before?

686. What are the current or emerging trends of culture?

687. Are you working on the right risks?

688. Is the customer technically sophisticated in the product area?

689. How would you assess the risk management process in the Applied behavior analysis project?

690. Is security a central objective?

691. Do you have a consistent repeatable process that is actually used?

692. How will economic events and trends likely affect the Applied behavior analysis project?

693. Do the people have the right combinations of skills?

694. What are the probable external agencies to act as Applied behavior analysis project manager?

695. Which phase of the Applied behavior analysis project do you take part in?

696. During which risk management process is a determination to transfer a risk made?

697. How risk averse are you?

698. What can go wrong?

699. How should you structure risks?

2.35 Risk Data Sheet: Applied behavior analysis

700. What were the Causes that contributed?

701. What do people affected think about the need for, and practicality of preventive measures?

702. How reliable is the data source?

703. What is the likelihood of it happening?

704. Whom do you serve (customers)?

705. Has a sensitivity analysis been carried out?

706. What can happen?

707. Potential for recurrence?

708. What are the main opportunities available to you that you should grab while you can?

709. Who has a vested interest in how you perform as your organization (our stakeholders)?

710. What are you trying to achieve (Objectives)?

711. How can it happen?

712. What actions can be taken to eliminate or remove risk?

713. During work activities could hazards exist?

714. What do you know?

2.36 Procurement Management Plan: Applied behavior analysis

715. Are meeting minutes captured and sent out after meetings?

716. Are there checklists created to determine if all quality processes are followed?

717. Are the Applied behavior analysis project plans updated on a frequent basis?

718. Was the scope definition used in task sequencing?

719. Have all involved Applied behavior analysis project stakeholders and work groups committed to the Applied behavior analysis project?

720. Have the key elements of a coherent Applied behavior analysis project management strategy been established?

721. What is the last item a Applied behavior analysis project manager must do to finalize Applied behavior analysis project close-out?

722. What were things that you did very well and want to do the same again on the next Applied behavior analysis project?

723. Are risk triggers captured?

724. Is Applied behavior analysis project work proceeding in accordance with the original Applied behavior analysis project schedule?

725. Is Applied behavior analysis project status reviewed with the steering and executive teams at appropriate intervals?

726. Is there a formal set of procedures supporting Stakeholder Management?

727. Is there an onboarding process in place?

728. Have all team members been part of identifying risks?

2.37 Source Selection Criteria: Applied behavior analysis

729. What should clarifications include?

730. What should a Draft Request for Proposal (DRFP) include?

731. Have team members been adequately trained?

732. What should communications be used to accomplish?

733. What documentation is necessary regarding electronic communications?

734. What is the last item a Applied behavior analysis project manager must do to finalize Applied behavior analysis project close-out?

735. When is it appropriate to conduct a preproposal conference?

736. How can the methods of publicizing the buy be tailored to yield more effective price competition?

737. How important is cost in the source selection decision relative to past performance and technical considerations?

738. What are the most common types of rating systems?

739. Do you want to have them collaborate at subfactor level?

740. Is experience evaluated?

741. What is the role of counsel in the procurement process?

742. What are the requirements for publicizing a RFP?

743. What should be considered?

744. What should a DRFP include?

745. Are there any common areas of weaknesses or deficiencies in the proposals in the competitive range?

746. What information is to be provided and when should it be provided?

747. Are resultant proposal revisions allowed?

748. What evidence should be provided regarding proposal evaluations?

2.38 Stakeholder Management Plan: Applied behavior analysis

749. Have all involved Applied behavior analysis project stakeholders and work groups committed to the Applied behavior analysis project?

750. Are procurement deliverables arriving on time and to specification?

751. Have key stakeholders been identified?

752. Have activity relationships and interdependencies within tasks been adequately identified?

753. Which of the records created within the Applied behavior analysis project, if any, does the Business Owner require access to?

754. How is information analyzed, and what specific pieces of data would be of interest to the Applied behavior analysis project manager?

755. Is the Applied behavior analysis project sponsor clearly communicating the business case or rationale for why this Applied behavior analysis project is needed?

756. Are decisions captured in a decisions log?

757. Are corrective actions and variances reported?

758. Are Applied behavior analysis project contact logs kept up to date?

759. What are the criteria for selecting other suppliers, including subcontractors?

760. Who is gathering information?

761. What procedures will be utilised to ensure effective monitoring of Applied behavior analysis project progress?

762. In your opinion, do certain Applied behavior analysis project resources hold a higher importance than other resources?

763. Are you meeting your customers expectations consistently?

2.39 Change Management Plan: Applied behavior analysis

764. What roles within your organization are affected, and how?

765. What skills, education, knowledge, or work experiences should the resources have for each identified competency?

766. Will all field readiness criteria have been practically met prior to training roll-out?

767. Is a training information sheet available?

768. What are the current methods of sharing information and do there need to be new ones developed?

769. Are work location changes required?

770. What are the major changes to processes?

771. Has this been negotiated with the customer and sponsor?

772. Is there a support model for this application and are the details available for distribution?

773. Has a training need analysis been carried out?

774. Who might present the most resistance?

775. Will you need new processes?

776. Why would a Applied behavior analysis project run more smoothly when change management is emphasized from the beginning?

777. What relationships will change?

778. Who might be able to help you the most?

779. Is there support for this application(s) and are the details available for distribution?

780. What risks may occur upfront?

781. What are the essentials of the message?

3.0 Executing Process Group: Applied behavior analysis

782. Does the Applied behavior analysis project team have enough people to execute the Applied behavior analysis project plan?

783. How will you avoid scope creep?

784. What are the critical steps involved in selecting measures and initiatives?

785. What areas were overlooked on this Applied behavior analysis project?

786. Is the Applied behavior analysis project making progress in helping to achieve the set results?

787. Is activity definition the first process involved in Applied behavior analysis project time management?

788. What are the main types of contracts if you do decide to outsource?

789. Contingency planning. if a risk event occurs, what will you do?

790. What are crucial elements of successful Applied behavior analysis project plan execution?

791. What will you do to minimize the impact should a risk event occur?

792. Who will be the main sponsor?

793. What type of information goes in the quality assurance plan?

794. What is the difference between conceptual, application, and evaluative questions?

795. How could you control progress of your Applied behavior analysis project?

796. Do the products created live up to the necessary quality?

797. Are escalated issues resolved promptly?

798. Does software appear easy to learn?

799. Could a new application negatively affect the current IT infrastructure?

800. Measurable - are the targets measurable?

3.1 Team Member Status Report: Applied behavior analysis

801. When a teams productivity and success depend on collaboration and the efficient flow of information, what generally fails them?

802. Does your organization have the means (staff, money, contract, etc.) to produce or to acquire the product, good, or service?

803. What specific interest groups do you have in place?

804. Does every department have to have a Applied behavior analysis project Manager on staff?

805. How it is to be done?

806. Why is it to be done?

807. How does this product, good, or service meet the needs of the Applied behavior analysis project and your organization as a whole?

808. Are the products of your organizations Applied behavior analysis projects meeting customers objectives?

809. Will the staff do training or is that done by a third party?

810. How much risk is involved?

811. Are the attitudes of staff regarding Applied behavior analysis project work improving?

812. Are your organizations Applied behavior analysis projects more successful over time?

813. How will resource planning be done?

814. Is there evidence that staff is taking a more professional approach toward management of your organizations Applied behavior analysis projects?

815. The problem with Reward & Recognition Programs is that the truly deserving people all too often get left out. How can you make it practical?

816. Do you have an Enterprise Applied behavior analysis project Management Office (EPMO)?

817. What is to be done?

818. How can you make it practical?

819. Does the product, good, or service already exist within your organization?

3.2 Change Request: Applied behavior analysis

820. What must be taken into consideration when introducing change control programs?

821. Who needs to approve change requests?

822. Does the schedule include Applied behavior analysis project management time and change request analysis time?

823. Screen shots or attachments included in a Change Request?

824. Will new change requests be acknowledged in a timely manner?

825. Where do changes come from?

826. What mechanism is used to appraise others of changes that are made?

827. Should staff call into the helpdesk or go to the website?

828. Who can suggest changes?

829. Will all change requests be unconditionally tracked through this process?

830. How do team members communicate with each other?

831. Are change requests logged and managed?

832. Have scm procedures for noting the change, recording it, and reporting it been followed?

833. How are the measures for carrying out the change established?

834. Who is responsible for the implementation and monitoring of all measures?

835. What are the duties of the change control team?

836. Since there are no change requests in your Applied behavior analysis project at this point, what must you have before you begin?

837. How to get changes (code) out in a timely manner?

838. How are changes graded and who is responsible for the rating?

839. Who is responsible to authorize changes?

3.3 Change Log: Applied behavior analysis

840. Does the suggested change request represent a desired enhancement to the products functionality?

841. Is the change request within Applied behavior analysis project scope?

842. Do the described changes impact on the integrity or security of the system?

843. Is this a mandatory replacement?

844. Is the submitted change a new change or a modification of a previously approved change?

845. Will the Applied behavior analysis project fail if the change request is not executed?

846. How does this relate to the standards developed for specific business processes?

847. Is the change request open, closed or pending?

848. How does this change affect scope?

849. Should a more thorough impact analysis be conducted?

850. When was the request submitted?

851. When was the request approved?

852. Is the change backward compatible without limitations?

853. How does this change affect the timeline of the schedule?

854. Does the suggested change request seem to represent a necessary enhancement to the product?

855. Who initiated the change request?

856. Is the requested change request a result of changes in other Applied behavior analysis project(s)?

3.4 Decision Log: Applied behavior analysis

857. Which variables make a critical difference?

858. Decision-making process; how will the team make decisions?

859. Who will be given a copy of this document and where will it be kept?

860. What was the rationale for the decision?

861. Linked to original objective?

862. What is the line where eDiscovery ends and document review begins?

863. Does anything need to be adjusted?

864. What eDiscovery problem or issue did your organization set out to fix or make better?

865. What are the cost implications?

866. Is your opponent open to a non-traditional workflow, or will it likely challenge anything you do?

867. How do you know when you are achieving it?

868. Is everything working as expected?

869. Do strategies and tactics aimed at less than full

control reduce the costs of management or simply shift the cost burden?

870. How consolidated and comprehensive a story can you tell by capturing currently available incident data in a central location and through a log of key decisions during an incident?

871. How does provision of information, both in terms of content and presentation, influence acceptance of alternative strategies?

872. How do you define success?

873. What is your overall strategy for quality control / quality assurance procedures?

874. With whom was the decision shared or considered?

875. It becomes critical to track and periodically revisit both operational effectiveness; Are you noticing all that you need to, and are you interpreting what you see effectively?

876. How does an increasing emphasis on cost containment influence the strategies and tactics used?

3.5 Quality Audit: Applied behavior analysis

877. How does your organization know that its staff embody the core knowledge, skills and characteristics for which it wishes to be recognized?

878. How does your organization know that its relationship with its (past) staff is appropriately effective and constructive?

879. How does your organization know that its management system is appropriately effective and constructive?

880. What does an analysis of your organizations staff profile suggest in terms of its planning, and how is this being addressed?

881. How does your organization know that its system for ensuring a positive organizational climate is appropriately effective and constructive?

882. Do the acceptance procedures and specifications include the criteria for acceptance/rejection, define the process to be used, and specify the measuring and test equipment that is to be used?

883. How does your organization know that its general support services planning and management systems are appropriately effective and constructive?

884. Are all complaints involving the possible failure

of a device, labeling, or packaging to meet any of its specifications reviewed, evaluated, and investigated?

885. Are training programs documented?

886. How does your organization know that its Mission, Vision and Values Statements are appropriate and effectively guiding your organization?

887. Is the continuing professional education of key personnel account fored in detail?

888. Are there appropriate indicators for monitoring the effectiveness and efficiency of processes?

889. How does your organization know that the range and quality of its accommodation, catering and transportation services are appropriately effective and constructive?

890. Have the risks associated with the intentions been identified, analyzed and appropriate responses developed?

891. How does your organization know that the research supervision provided to its staff is appropriately effective and constructive?

892. Have personnel cleanliness and health requirements been established?

893. Can your organization demonstrate exactly how and why results were achieved?

894. How does your organization know that its information technology system is serving its needs as

effectively and constructively as is appropriate?

895. Are the review comments incorporated?

896. How does your organization know that its relationships with industry and employers are appropriately effective and constructive?

3.6 Team Directory: Applied behavior analysis

897. Do purchase specifications and configurations match requirements?

898. Process decisions: do invoice amounts match accepted work in place?

899. When does information need to be distributed?

900. How do unidentified risks impact the outcome of the Applied behavior analysis project?

901. What needs to be communicated?

902. Process decisions: are contractors adequately prosecuting the work?

903. Who will talk to the customer?

904. Why is the work necessary?

905. Process decisions: how well was task order work performed?

906. When will you produce deliverables?

907. Who will be the stakeholders on your next Applied behavior analysis project?

908. Contract requirements complied with?

909. Who are the Team Members?

910. Decisions: what could be done better to improve the quality of the constructed product?

911. Who will report Applied behavior analysis project status to all stakeholders?

912. Process decisions: is work progressing on schedule and per contract requirements?

913. Process decisions: which organizational elements and which individuals will be assigned management functions?

914. Process decisions: are there any statutory or regulatory issues relevant to the timely execution of work?

3.7 Team Operating Agreement: Applied behavior analysis

915. Must your team members rely on the expertise of other members to complete tasks?

916. What administrative supports will be put in place to support the team and the teams supervisor?

917. What types of accommodations will be formulated and put in place for sustaining the team?

918. Communication protocols: how will the team communicate?

919. Is compensation based on team and individual performance?

920. Do you ensure that all participants know how to use the required technology?

921. What are the boundaries (organizational or geographic) within which you operate?

922. How do you want to be thought of and known within your organization?

923. Are there the right people on your team?

924. Did you determine the technology methods that best match the messages to be communicated?

925. What is your unique contribution to your

organization?

926. Do you upload presentation materials in advance and test the technology?

927. Are team roles clearly defined and accepted?

928. Methodologies: how will key team processes be implemented, such as training, research, work deliverable production, review and approval processes, knowledge management, and meeting procedures?

929. How will group handle unplanned absences?

930. Do you use a parking lot for any items that are important and outside of the agenda?

931. What resources can be provided for the team in terms of equipment, space, time for training, protected time and space for meetings, and travel allowances?

932. To whom do you deliver your services?

933. Do team members need to frequently communicate as a full group to make timely decisions?

934. How will you resolve conflict efficiently and respectfully?

3.8 Team Performance Assessment: Applied behavior analysis

935. To what degree are sub-teams possible or necessary?

936. How do you manage human resources?

937. When does the medium matter?

938. To what degree does the teams purpose constitute a broader, deeper aspiration than just accomplishing short-term goals?

939. Social categorization and intergroup behaviour: Does minimal intergroup discrimination make social identity more positive?

940. Effects of crew composition on crew performance: Does the whole equal the sum of its parts?

941. To what degree will new and supplemental skills be introduced as the need is recognized?

942. To what degree are the skill areas critical to team performance present?

943. Lack of method variance in self-reported affect and perceptions at work: Reality or artifact?

944. What structural changes have you made or are you preparing to make?

945. To what degree is the team cognizant of small wins to be celebrated along the way?

946. If you are worried about method variance before you collect data, what sort of design elements might you include to reduce or eliminate the threat of method variance?

947. To what degree do team members agree with the goals, relative importance, and the ways in which achievement will be measured?

948. To what degree are the goals realistic?

949. Do you promptly inform members about major developments that may affect them?

950. To what degree will the team ensure that all members equitably share the work essential to the success of the team?

951. To what degree do team members feel that the purpose of the team is important, if not exciting?

952. To what degree does the teams work approach provide opportunity for members to engage in results-based evaluation?

953. If you have received criticism from reviewers that your work suffered from method variance, what was the circumstance?

954. To what degree can all members engage in open and interactive considerations?

3.9 Team Member Performance Assessment: Applied behavior analysis

955. To what degree do members articulate the goals beyond the team membership?

956. How accurately is your plan implemented?

957. What are the standards or expectations for success?

958. What is needed for effective data teams?

959. What is a general description of the processes under performance measurement and assessment?

960. What changes do you need to make to align practices with beliefs?

961. Should a ratee get a copy of all the raters documents about the employees performance?

962. What are best practices in use for the performance measurement system?

963. Which training platform formats (i.e., mobile, virtual, videogame-based) were implemented in your effort(s)?

964. Are there any safeguards to prevent intentional or unintentional rating errors?

965. Does adaptive training work?

966. How should adaptive assessments be implemented?

967. How are assessments designed, delivered, and otherwise used to maximize training?

968. What is a significant fact or event?

969. What is the Business Management Oversight Process?

970. Did training work?

971. New skills/knowledge gained this year?

972. How is performance assessment used in making future award decisions including options and extend/compete decisions?

3.10 Issue Log: Applied behavior analysis

973. Are there too many who have an interest in some aspect of your work?

974. In your work, how much time is spent on stakeholder identification?

975. What are the typical contents?

976. Can an impact cause deviation beyond team, stage or Applied behavior analysis project tolerances?

977. Are stakeholder roles recognized by your organization?

978. Why not more evaluators?

979. Are they needed?

980. Who is the stakeholder?

981. How often do you engage with stakeholders?

982. Do you often overlook a key stakeholder or stakeholder group?

983. What is the stakeholders level of authority?

984. What is the impact on the risks?

985. Is access to the Issue Log controlled?

986. What approaches do you use?

987. Who are the members of the governing body?

4.0 Monitoring and Controlling Process Group: Applied behavior analysis

988. How many potential communications channels exist on the Applied behavior analysis project?

989. Is there sufficient time allotted between the general system design and the detailed system design phases?

990. Accuracy: what design will lead to accurate information?

991. How many more potential communications channels were introduced by the discovery of the new stakeholders?

992. Did the Applied behavior analysis project team have enough people to execute the Applied behavior analysis project plan?

993. Did you implement the program as designed?

994. What were things that you need to improve?

995. Is the program in place as intended?

996. Do clients benefit (change) from the services?

997. How should needs be met?

998. How well did the chosen processes produce the

expected results?

999. How is agile program management done?

1000. Who needs to be involved in the planning?

1001. What are the deliverables?

1002. Who needs to be engaged upfront to ensure use of results?

1003. What business situation is being addressed?

1004. Feasibility: how much money, time, and effort can you put into this?

4.1 Project Performance Report: Applied behavior analysis

1005. To what degree do team members articulate the teams work approach?

1006. To what degree does the teams work approach provide opportunity for members to engage in fact-based problem solving?

1007. To what degree does the teams work approach provide opportunity for members to engage in open interaction?

1008. To what degree do the relationships of the informal organization motivate taskrelevant behavior and facilitate task completion?

1009. To what degree does the teams approach to its work allow for modification and improvement over time?

1010. To what degree does the information network provide individuals with the information they require?

1011. To what degree are the teams goals and objectives clear, simple, and measurable?

1012. To what degree are the structures of the formal organization consistent with the behaviors in the informal organization?

1013. To what degree are the tasks requirements

reflected in the flow and storage of information?

1014. How can Applied behavior analysis project sustainability be maintained?

1015. To what degree will the team adopt a concrete, clearly understood, and agreed-upon approach that will result in achievement of the teams goals?

1016. To what degree is the information network consistent with the structure of the formal organization?

1017. To what degree does the task meet individual needs?

1018. To what degree will team members, individually and collectively, commit time to help themselves and others learn and develop skills?

1019. What is in it for you?

4.2 Variance Analysis: Applied behavior analysis

1020. Why do variances exist?

1021. Are procedures for variance analysis documented and consistently applied at the control account level and selected WBS and organizational levels at least monthly as a routine task?

1022. What can be the cause of an increase in costs?

1023. What does a favorable labor efficiency variance mean?

1024. How do you manage changes in the nature of the overhead requirements?

1025. Did your organization lose existing customers and/or gain new customers?

1026. Are overhead costs budgets established on a basis consistent with the anticipated direct business base?

1027. How do you verify authorization to proceed with all authorized work?

1028. Do you identify potential or actual budget-based and time-based schedule variances?

1029. What is the dollar amount of the fluctuation?

1030. What is the total budget for the Applied behavior analysis project (including estimates for authorized and unpriced work)?

1031. Is there a logical explanation for any variance?

1032. Are estimates of costs at completion generated in a rational, consistent manner?

1033. What is the actual cost of work performed?

1034. Are control accounts opened and closed based on the start and completion of work contained therein?

1035. What are the actual costs to date?

4.3 Earned Value Status: Applied behavior analysis

1036. When is it going to finish?

1037. Verification is a process of ensuring that the developed system satisfies the stakeholders agreements and specifications; Are you building the product right? What do you verify?

1038. Earned value can be used in almost any Applied behavior analysis project situation and in almost any Applied behavior analysis project environment. it may be used on large Applied behavior analysis projects, medium sized Applied behavior analysis projects, tiny Applied behavior analysis projects (in cut-down form), complex and simple Applied behavior analysis projects and in any market sector. some people, of course, know all about earned value, they have used it for years - but perhaps not as effectively as they could have?

1039. How much is it going to cost by the finish?

1040. What is the unit of forecast value?

1041. Where are your problem areas?

1042. If earned value management (EVM) is so good in determining the true status of a Applied behavior analysis project and Applied behavior analysis project its completion, why is it that hardly any one uses it in information systems related Applied behavior analysis projects?

1043. Where is evidence-based earned value in your organization reported?

1044. Validation is a process of ensuring that the developed system will actually achieve the stakeholders desired outcomes; Are you building the right product? What do you validate?

1045. Are you hitting your Applied behavior analysis projects targets?

1046. How does this compare with other Applied behavior analysis projects?

4.4 Risk Audit: Applied behavior analysis

1047. Are risk management strategies documented?

1048. Can assurance be expanded beyond the traditional audit without undermining independence?

1049. Whence the business risk audit?

1050. What is the effect of globalisation; is business becoming too complex and can the auditor rely on auditing standards?

1051. Do staff understand the extent of duty of care?

1052. Are auditors able to effectively apply more soft evidence found in the risk-assessment process with the results of more tangible audit evidence found through more substantive testing?

1053. Is the process supported by tools?

1054. What are the boundaries of the auditors responsibility for policing management fidelity?

1055. When your organization is entering into a major contract, does it seek legal advice?

1056. What is happening in other jurisdictions? Could that happen here?

1057. Does the team have the right mix of skills?

1058. Number of users of the product?

1059. Are policies communicated to all affected?

1060. Risks with Applied behavior analysis projects or new initiatives?

1061. What are risks and how do you manage them?

1062. Are regular safety inspections made of buildings, grounds and equipment?

1063. What are the benefits of a Enterprise wide approach to Risk Management?

1064. Does your board meet regularly and document all decisions and actions?

1065. What are the strategic implications with clients when auditors focus audit resources based on business-level risks?

4.5 Contractor Status Report: Applied behavior analysis

1066. What is the average response time for answering a support call?

1067. How does the proposed individual meet each requirement?

1068. What are the minimum and optimal bandwidth requirements for the proposed solution?

1069. Describe how often regular updates are made to the proposed solution. Are corresponding regular updates included in the standard maintenance plan?

1070. What was the actual budget or estimated cost for your organizations services?

1071. What was the final actual cost?

1072. What was the overall budget or estimated cost?

1073. How long have you been using the services?

1074. Who can list a Applied behavior analysis project as organization experience, your organization or a previous employee of your organization?

1075. How is risk transferred?

1076. Are there contractual transfer concerns?

1077. What process manages the contracts?

1078. What was the budget or estimated cost for your organizations services?

1079. If applicable; describe your standard schedule for new software version releases. Are new software version releases included in the standard maintenance plan?

4.6 Formal Acceptance: Applied behavior analysis

1080. What lessons were learned about your Applied behavior analysis project management methodology?

1081. Does it do what Applied behavior analysis project team said it would?

1082. What function(s) does it fill or meet?

1083. Was the Applied behavior analysis project work done on time, within budget, and according to specification?

1084. Do you perform formal acceptance or burn-in tests?

1085. What are the requirements against which to test, Who will execute?

1086. What features, practices, and processes proved to be strengths or weaknesses?

1087. What can you do better next time?

1088. Did the Applied behavior analysis project manager and team act in a professional and ethical manner?

1089. Was the Applied behavior analysis project managed well?

1090. Who would use it?

1091. Was business value realized?

1092. Do you buy-in installation services?

1093. Did the Applied behavior analysis project achieve its MOV?

1094. Do you buy pre-configured systems or build your own configuration?

1095. Was the Applied behavior analysis project goal achieved?

1096. Who supplies data?

1097. Have all comments been addressed?

1098. Does it do what client said it would?

1099. General estimate of the costs and times to complete the Applied behavior analysis project?

5.0 Closing Process Group: Applied behavior analysis

1100. If action is called for, what form should it take?

1101. What could be done to improve the process?

1102. What were the desired outcomes?

1103. Were cost budgets met?

1104. What could have been improved?

1105. Who are the Applied behavior analysis project stakeholders?

1106. What is the amount of funding and what Applied behavior analysis project phases are funded?

1107. Mitigate. what will you do to minimize the impact should a risk event occur?

1108. What is the Applied behavior analysis project Management Process?

1109. Did the Applied behavior analysis project team have enough people to execute the Applied behavior analysis project plan?

1110. Were the outcomes different from the already stated planned?

1111. What is an Encumbrance?

1112. What can you do better next time, and what specific actions can you take to improve?

1113. When will the Applied behavior analysis project be done?

5.1 Procurement Audit: Applied behavior analysis

1114. Was the payment made to the supplier/contractor within the time frames indicated in the contracts?

1115. Are behaviour modification applied to change procurement of goods and services if procurement is not functioning properly?

1116. Access to data, including standing data, and the identification of restriction levels and authorised personnel was in place?

1117. Is there no evidence that the consultants participating in the Applied behavior analysis project design released information to contractors competing for the prime contract?

1118. Were there no material changes in the contract shortly after award?

1119. Was suitability of candidates accurately assessed?

1120. Does the strategy ensure that needs are met, and not exceeded?

1121. Was the tender clearly and properly specified, including evaluation criteria and knowing about the market and therefore not over-prescriptive and receptive to innovation?

1122. Was the formal review of requests to participate or evaluation of bids correctly undertaken?

1123. Is the opportunity properly published?

1124. Are there procedures for trade-in arrangements?

1125. Does the individual approving disbursements sign or initial the document?

1126. Does procurement staff have recognized professional procurement qualifications or sufficient training?

1127. Are required quality and service standards set?

1128. Are the established budget and timetable (milestones) respected?

1129. How do you avoid delays at any stage/ stages of the procurement process?

1130. Is there a formal program of inservice training for personnel in the business management function?

1131. Is there a policy covering the relationship of other departments with vendors?

1132. Is it clear which procurement procedure your organization has opted for?

1133. Are fixed asset values recorded at historical cost?

5.2 Contract Close-Out: Applied behavior analysis

1134. How is the contracting office notified of the automatic contract close-out?

1135. Change in circumstances?

1136. Why Outsource?

1137. Have all contracts been completed?

1138. Was the contract sufficiently clear so as not to result in numerous disputes and misunderstandings?

1139. What happens to the recipient of services?

1140. Change in knowledge?

1141. Was the contract type appropriate?

1142. Has each contract been audited to verify acceptance and delivery?

1143. Have all acceptance criteria been met prior to final payment to contractors?

1144. Was the contract complete without requiring numerous changes and revisions?

1145. Change in attitude or behavior?

1146. Have all contract records been included in the

Applied behavior analysis project archives?

1147. Are the signers the authorized officials?

1148. Parties: Authorized?

1149. Parties: who is involved?

1150. How/when used ?

1151. How does it work?

1152. What is capture management?

1153. Have all contracts been closed?

5.3 Project or Phase Close-Out: Applied behavior analysis

1154. Is there a clear cause and effect between the activity and the lesson learned?

1155. How much influence did the stakeholder have over others?

1156. Does the lesson educate others to improve performance?

1157. Planned remaining costs?

1158. In preparing the Lessons Learned report, should it reflect a consensus viewpoint, or should the report reflect the different individual viewpoints?

1159. Was the user/client satisfied with the end product?

1160. Which changes might a stakeholder be required to make as a result of the Applied behavior analysis project?

1161. Who exerted influence that has positively affected or negatively impacted the Applied behavior analysis project?

1162. Who is responsible for award close-out?

1163. What were the goals and objectives of the communications strategy for the Applied behavior analysis project?

1164. When and how were information needs best met?

1165. Have business partners been involved extensively, and what data was required for them?

1166. Complete yes or no?

1167. Can the lesson learned be replicated?

1168. What benefits or impacts does the stakeholder group expect to obtain as a result of the Applied behavior analysis project?

1169. Did the delivered product meet the specified requirements and goals of the Applied behavior analysis project?

1170. In addition to assessing whether the Applied behavior analysis project was successful, it is equally critical to analyze why it was or was not fully successful. Are you including this?

1171. What is a Risk Management Process?

1172. What was the preferred delivery mechanism?

5.4 Lessons Learned: Applied behavior analysis

1173. Overall, how effective were the efforts to prepare you and your organization for the impact of the product/service of the Applied behavior analysis project?

1174. What were the major enablers to a quick response?

1175. How effective was the training you received in preparation for the use of the product/service?

1176. What is below the surface?

1177. What if anything has been lacking?

1178. How useful do individuals find communications?

1179. What were the actual outcomes?

1180. Were any strategies or activities unsuccessful?

1181. What report generation capability is needed?

1182. Was any formal risk assessment carried out at the start of the Applied behavior analysis project, and was this followed up during the Applied behavior analysis project?

1183. What is the fiscal dependency?

1184. What specialization does the task require?

1185. What worked well?

1186. How smooth do you feel Integration has been?

1187. What is the desired end-state?

1188. What worked well or did not work well, either for this Applied behavior analysis project or for the Applied behavior analysis project team?

1189. What would you change?

1190. How effective were Best Practices & Lessons Learned from prior Applied behavior analysis projects utilized in this Applied behavior analysis project?

1191. What are the expectations of the individuals?

Index

ability 32, 87
abnormal   189
absence   87
absences   235
accept   174
acceptable   54, 81, 103, 128, 145
acceptance   8, 118, 145, 147, 151, 228-229, 254, 260
accepted   111, 152, 185, 232, 235
access 4, 10-12, 21, 76, 142, 192, 215, 240, 258
accomplish   10, 80, 109, 114, 163, 188, 213
accordance   177, 212
according   35, 42, 180, 204, 254
account   37, 59, 156, 174, 188, 230, 246
accounting   157, 194
accounts   156, 247
accuracy   52, 151, 197, 242
accurate   12, 120, 146, 242
accurately   238, 258
achieve   10, 73, 82, 85, 122, 163, 191-192, 209, 219, 249, 255
achieved   25, 77, 88, 118, 230, 255
achieving   227
acquire   221
acquired   162, 192
across 53
action 53, 97, 99, 101-102, 139, 150, 203, 256
actionable   55, 111
actions 18, 56, 94, 96, 156, 201, 204, 209, 215, 251, 257
active 180
actively   199
activities   25-26, 45, 83, 93, 102, 110, 138, 144, 160-161, 163-164, 167-168, 171, 173, 175, 178, 181, 196, 210, 264
activity 5-6, 34-35, 139, 159, 161, 163-169, 173, 181-182, 215, 219, 262
actual 34, 55, 145, 156-157, 177, 193-194, 246-247, 252, 264
actually   34, 66, 87, 99, 187, 207, 249
adaptive   239
addition   263
additional   31, 42, 67, 72-73, 183
additions   98

address   1, 24, 91, 113, 177
addressed   141, 169, 203, 229, 243, 255
addressing   32, 111
adequate   42, 140, 142-143
adequately   42, 189, 213, 215, 232
adjust 103
adjusted   97, 227
adopted   138
advance   203, 235
advantage   1, 73, 108
advantages   118
adverse   156
advice 250
advise 2
affect 68, 75, 115, 123, 139, 148, 151, 179, 181, 203, 207, 220, 225-226, 236-237
affected   136-137, 159, 179, 209, 217, 251, 262
affecting   14, 28, 75, 139
afford 204
affordable   79
against 40, 103, 157, 254
agencies   205, 208
agenda   235
agents 191
aggregate   53
agreed   159
Agreement   8, 127, 234
agreements   61, 80, 197, 248
agrees 110
alerts   93
aligned   27
Alignment   159
alleged   3
alliance   89
allocate   109, 156, 181
allocated   56, 59, 113
allocating   156-157
allotted   242
allowable   55
allowances   235
allowed   2, 124, 171, 214
allows 12, 167
almost 248

already 156, 188, 190, 222, 256
altogether 206
always 12
amended 187
amount 28, 246, 256
amounts 232
amplify 72, 109
analysis 3-9, 11-16, 18-76, 78-97, 99-140, 142-144, 146, 148, 150-154, 156, 159-161, 163, 165, 167-169, 171-189, 191, 193-195, 197-201, 203-209, 211-213, 215-227, 229, 232-234, 236, 238, 240, 242, 244-252, 254-258, 260-265
analyze 4, 61, 68, 72, 263
analyzed 93, 132, 151, 215, 230
another 155, 164
answer 13-14, 18, 30, 46, 61, 77, 93, 105
answered 29, 45, 60, 76, 92, 104, 129
answering 13, 165, 252
anybody 138
anyone 42, 110, 128
anything 162, 170, 181, 227, 264
appear 3, 220
applicable 13, 178, 189, 194, 253
Applied 3-16, 18-76, 78-97, 99-140, 142-144, 146, 148, 150-154, 156, 159-161, 163, 165, 167-169, 171-183, 185-189, 191, 193, 195, 197-201, 203-209, 211-213, 215-227, 229, 232-234, 236, 238, 240, 242, 244-252, 254-258, 260-265
appointed 33, 44
appointing 205
appraise 223
appreciate 196
approach 84, 91, 116, 118, 137, 152, 222, 237, 244-245, 251
approaches 78, 85, 199, 241
approval 35, 125, 235
approve 223
approved 41, 65, 132, 148, 173, 187, 197, 225
approving 148, 187, 259
Architects 10
archives 261
around 112, 115, 194
arriving 215
articulate 238, 244
artifact 236
asking 3, 10, 185, 191

aspect 240
aspects 165
aspiration 236
assess 28, 85, 101, 123, 167, 207
assessed 87, 204, 258
assessing 78, 95, 263
assessment 7-8, 11-12, 27, 142, 144, 160, 196, 205, 236, 238-239, 264
assets 55
assign 28
assigned 31, 37, 140, 150, 154, 156, 159, 179, 193, 233
Assignment 6, 193
assist 11, 69, 98, 184
assistant 10
associated 131, 230
assuming 206
Assumption 5, 152
assurance 142-143, 151, 179, 196-197, 220, 228, 250
attached 176
attainable 40, 174
attempted 42
attempting 94
attend 26
attendance 43
attended 1, 44
attention 14, 110
attitude 260
attitudes 222
Attributes 5, 163, 189
audited 197, 260
auditing 22, 96, 121, 153, 250
auditor 250
auditors 250-251
author 3
authorised 258
authority 72, 144, 240
authorize 224
authorized 140, 157, 193, 246-247, 261
automatic 260
available 23, 25, 38, 42, 53, 67-68, 79, 98, 108, 131, 162, 164, 188-189, 201, 203, 205, 209, 217-218, 228
Average 14, 29, 45, 60, 76, 92, 104, 129, 175, 252
averse 208

background 12, 134
backing 137
backup 150
backward 226
balanced 80
bandwidth 252
barriers 108
Baseline 6, 128, 140, 185
baselined 143, 159-160
basics 125
because 2, 182
become 106, 113, 125, 148
becomes 205, 228
becoming 250
before 1-2, 12, 42, 94, 161, 167-168, 197, 201, 207, 224, 237
beginning 4, 17, 29, 45, 60, 76, 92, 104, 129, 218
begins 227
behavior 3-9, 11-16, 18-76, 78-97, 99-140, 142-144, 146, 148, 150-154, 156, 159-161, 163, 165, 167-169, 171-183, 185-189, 191, 193, 195, 197-201, 203-209, 211-213, 215-227, 229, 232-234, 236, 238, 240, 242, 244-252, 254-258, 260-265
behaviors 27, 196, 244
behaviour 236, 258
behind 2
belief 13, 18, 30, 46, 61, 77, 93, 105, 122
beliefs 238
believe 2, 110, 122, 132
benchmark 190
benefit 3, 20, 22, 24, 59, 104, 180, 194, 242
benefits 19, 50, 52-53, 63, 72, 105-106, 118, 124-125, 251, 263
better 10, 30, 50, 82, 175, 183, 202, 227, 233, 254, 257
between 148, 152, 158, 160, 179, 194, 200, 220, 242, 262
beyond 238, 240, 250
bidders 145
biggest 58, 88, 181, 190
blinding 65
bother 52
bottleneck 175
bounce 68, 75
boundaries 42, 234, 250
bounds 42
Breakdown 5-6, 154, 171

briefed 33
brings 35
broader 236
broken 76
budget 2, 101, 109, 138, 140, 142-143, 156, 175, 177, 181-182, 247, 252-254, 259
budgeted 55
budgets 19, 110, 157, 246, 256
building 18, 102, 133, 152, 171, 248-249
buildings 251
burden 228
burn-in 254
business 2, 10, 12, 20-21, 33, 57, 59, 68, 76, 84-86, 99, 109, 113, 115, 118-119, 122, 125, 128, 131-132, 140, 144, 146, 150, 158, 190, 205, 215, 225, 239, 243, 246, 250, 255, 259, 263
busywork 132
buy-in 108, 255
Calculate 166
called 256
candidates 258
cannot 156, 167, 178
capability 28, 153, 160, 264
capable 10, 32
capacities 128
capacity 18, 28, 86, 182
capital 121
capitalize 71
capture 55, 98, 261
captured 52, 73, 82, 120, 211, 215
capturing 228
career 148
careers 119
carried 63, 209, 217, 264
carrying 224
cash-drain 136
Cashflow 136
catching 1
categories 203
category 33
catering 230
caused 3, 48
causes 50, 53-54, 58, 61, 64, 70, 75, 94, 209
causing 28

celebrated 237
center 141
central 207, 228
centrally 80
certain 199, 216
certified 179
challenge 10, 227
challenges 132
change 7, 18, 24, 33, 47, 55, 66-68, 73, 81, 85, 88, 91, 98, 107, 113, 134-135, 154, 163, 167, 178, 180-181, 187, 189, 191, 202-203, 207, 217-218, 223-226, 242, 258, 260, 265
changed 26, 33, 87, 102, 110, 178, 183, 186
changes 19, 39, 41, 59, 65, 79-80, 94, 98, 107, 118, 127, 132-133, 140, 151-152, 157, 159, 173, 193-194, 217, 223-226, 236, 238, 246, 258, 260, 262
changing 103, 112, 136, 202
channels 242
charged 51
Charter 4, 44, 82, 133-134, 139, 198
charts 72
cheaper 50
checked 62, 96, 103
checklists 11, 143, 211
choice 33, 108
choices 173
choose 13, 78, 138
chosen 139, 242
circumvent 19
claimed 3
clarify 123
classes 180, 198
clearly 13, 18, 24, 30, 33, 37-38, 46, 61-62, 77, 87, 93, 105, 195-196, 215, 235, 245, 258
client 55, 121, 140, 255, 262
clients 33, 242, 251
climate 229
closed 95, 225, 247, 261
closely 12, 177
close-out 8, 211, 213, 260, 262
closest 106
Closing 8, 72, 256
Coaches 30, 37, 191
cognizant 237

coherent   160, 211
colleague   123
colleagues   121, 124
collect 100, 183, 192, 237
collected   30, 43, 65-67, 70, 73, 151
collection   67, 191
combine   85
coming   71
comments   231, 255
commercial   156
commit   197, 245
commitment   96, 109
committed   66, 152, 178, 187, 197, 211, 215
Committee   180, 197
common   143, 200, 213-214
community   183
companies   3, 102
company   1-2, 10, 50, 73, 109-110, 113, 120, 122-123, 128
compare   74, 89, 177, 249
compared   120
comparing   78, 156
comparison   13
compatible   226
compelling   32
compete   239
competency   217
competing   52, 258
competitor   2
compile   187
complain   190
complaints   204, 229
complete   3, 11, 13, 39, 42-43, 140, 159-161, 163, 165, 168, 175-176, 195, 203, 234, 255, 260, 263
completed   14, 31, 37-39, 167-168, 185, 260
completely   1
completing   114
completion   35, 38, 139, 150, 157, 168, 181, 244, 247-248
complex   10, 122, 188, 248, 250
complexity   22, 49, 69
compliance   1, 20, 51, 53, 56, 71, 80, 152, 187
complied   232
component   190
components   173, 197

comprise	138
compute	14
computer	153
concept	80
concepts	153, 188
conceptual	220
concern	49, 89
concerned	21
concerns	2, 23, 106, 252
concise	144
concrete	78, 245
condition	102, 138, 177
conditions	96, 118
conduct	159, 188, 213
conducted	142, 160, 179, 225
conducting	187
conference	213
confidence	190, 202
confident	168
confirm	13
conflict	235
conjure	146
connecting	106
consensus	262
consider	19, 26, 28
considered	21, 25, 52, 214, 228
considers	73
consistent	48, 71, 94, 140, 156, 207, 244-247
constantly	1
constitute	236
Constraint	5, 152
consult	1
consultant	1-2, 10, 181-182
consulted	116
consulting	2, 59
consumers	110
contact	10, 113-114, 216
contain	26, 61, 95
contained	3, 247
contains	11
content	37, 140, 228
contents	3-4, 11, 240
context	36, 39, 41, 174

continual 95, 100
continuing 230
continuity 57
continuous 74, 78
contract 8, 156, 168, 179-180, 193, 221, 232-233, 250, 258, 260
Contractor 8, 252, 258
contracts 35, 61, 156-157, 174, 219, 253, 258, 260-261
control 4, 44, 47, 61, 93-94, 96, 98, 100-101, 104, 156, 173, 184, 220, 223-224, 228, 246-247
controlled 64, 203, 240
controls 26, 62, 67, 92, 96-99, 204
convention 113
convey 3
convince 193
cooperate 184
Copyright 3
corporate 2
correct 46, 93, 178
correction 157
corrective 56, 94, 215
correctly 259
correspond 11-12
costing 53
counsel 214
counting 116, 145
counts 116
course 33, 55, 248
covering 11, 97, 259
coworker 121
craziest 117
create 21, 62, 108-109, 118
created 65, 72, 102, 135, 138-139, 143, 211, 215, 220
creating 10, 58
creative 25
creativity 90
credible 184
crisis 23
criteria 4, 7, 11-12, 33, 39-40, 64, 85, 89, 95, 108, 125, 130, 147, 149-150, 178, 184, 213, 216-217, 229, 258, 260
CRITERION 4, 18, 30, 46, 61, 77, 93, 105
critical 31, 37, 43, 72, 84, 94, 97, 116, 138, 165, 173, 175, 219, 227-228, 236, 263

critically 193
criticism 65, 237
cross-sell 107
crucial 75, 165, 219
crystal 13
culture 41, 75, 207
current 39, 46, 54, 57, 63, 73, 83, 87, 122, 125-127, 143, 168, 188, 193, 196, 198, 204, 207, 217, 220
currently 35, 116, 228
custom 18
customer 26, 31, 34, 41-43, 85, 100, 103, 107, 110, 112, 123, 142, 150, 188, 190, 205, 207, 217, 232
customers 3, 27, 33, 37, 49-50, 55, 63, 74, 95, 106-107, 109, 111, 114-115, 118, 120, 124, 126, 134, 147, 150, 202, 209, 216, 221, 246
customized 2
cut-down 248
cycles 134
damage 3
Dashboard 11
dashboards 98
databases 191
day-to-day 100, 106
deadlines 25
dealer 179
dealing 24
deceitful 121
decide 85, 174, 219
decided 78
deciding 114
decision 7, 54, 64, 82, 84, 89-91, 131-132, 213, 227-228
decisions 79, 83-85, 90-91, 97, 100, 103, 132, 215, 227-228, 232-233, 235, 239, 251
decomposed 173
dedicated 10
deeper 13, 236
defect 180, 198
define 4, 30, 35, 39, 41, 62, 74, 81, 143, 195, 228-229
defined 13, 18, 23, 26, 30-41, 46, 61, 64, 70, 77, 93, 105, 143, 150-152, 154, 159, 173-174, 178, 189, 194-196, 235
defines 19, 39-40, 171
defining 10, 117
definite 95

definition 24, 31-32, 38, 43, 153, 211, 219
degree 178, 202, 236-238, 244-245
-degree 2
delayed 166
delays 53, 161, 175, 259
delegated 32
deletions 98
deliver 27, 43, 85, 108, 118, 183, 235
delivered 56, 125, 185, 239, 263
delivering 204
delivery 20, 54, 118, 125, 165, 168, 260, 263
demand 117
department 10, 109, 221
depend 221
dependency 264
dependent 125
depends 110
depict 167
deploy 97, 118
deployed 97
deploying 59
deployment 48
derive 95
Describe 21, 144, 148, 252-253
described 3, 146, 225
describing 37
deserving 222
design 12, 66, 75, 79, 91, 116, 139, 153, 237, 242, 258
designed 10, 12, 73, 81, 239, 242
designing 10
desired 27, 42, 73, 84, 131, 173, 225, 249, 256, 265
detail 90, 143, 154, 163, 176, 230
detailed 62, 72, 138, 152, 178, 194, 242
details 58, 217-218
detect 96
determine 12, 115, 161, 174, 183, 211, 234
determined 65, 115, 134, 191-192
detracting 120
develop 58, 77, 82, 86-87, 140, 144, 154, 182, 245
developed 12, 38-39, 44, 59, 82, 153, 157, 180, 185, 188, 192, 217, 225, 230, 248-249
developer 206
developers 201

developing 74, 89, 138, 178, 194
deviation 240
device 230
diagram 5, 49, 54, 70, 167, 178
Diagrams 52, 188
Dictionary 5, 156
difference 138, 160, 220, 227
different 10, 19, 33-34, 37, 42, 69-70, 115, 121, 143, 152, 256, 262
difficult 66, 163, 168, 171, 173
dilemma 111
direct 193, 246
direction 33, 50
directly 3, 63, 74, 156, 199
Directory 8, 232
Disagree 13, 18, 30, 46, 61, 77, 93, 105
disaster 53, 57
disclosure 102
discovery 242
discussion 118
displayed 30, 69, 175
disputes 260
disqualify 66
disregard 174
disruptive 68
Divided 29, 32, 45, 60, 76, 92, 104, 129
document 12, 43, 146, 153, 227, 251, 259
documented 32, 81, 87, 94, 101-102, 147, 150-153, 157, 159, 179, 187, 195, 198, 230, 246, 250
documents 10, 152, 173, 238
dollar 246
domains 90
Driver 66
drivers 59, 76
drives 54
driving 109, 112
duration 6, 138-139, 154, 167, 173, 175
durations 34, 178
during 33, 86, 132, 143, 169, 208, 210, 228, 264
duties 224
dynamics 31
eagerly 2
earlier 124

earned 8, 173, 179, 248-249
economic 207
economical 114, 141
economies 136
economy 87
eDiscovery 227
edition 11
editorial 3
educate 262
educated 1
education 26, 102, 217, 230
effect 203, 250, 262
effective 19, 21, 111, 116, 201, 213, 216, 229-231, 238, 264-265
effects 51, 165, 199, 236
efficiency 74, 103, 230, 246
efficient 54, 87, 138, 221
effort 38, 49, 57, 118, 142, 156, 193, 238, 243
efforts 42, 83, 264
either 265
electronic 3, 213
element 156-157
elements 12, 68, 95, 115, 156, 158, 160, 193-194, 198, 211, 219, 233, 237
Elevator 146
elicit 191
eliminate 178, 209, 237
eliminated 193
embarking 32
embody 229
emerging 1, 66, 103, 207
emphasis 228
emphasized 218
employee 85, 119, 252
employees 21, 24, 27, 70, 111, 120, 124, 173, 238
employers 135, 231
empower 10
enable 68
enablers 112, 264
encourage 90
end-state 265
endure 182
energy 1

engage 237, 240, 244
engaged 243
engagement 55, 135
enhance 99
enhanced 119
enhancing 93
enough 10, 65, 110, 123-124, 146, 148, 179, 205, 219, 242, 256
ensure 34, 40, 75, 106, 113, 118, 125, 142, 153, 173, 182, 187, 191-192, 196, 198, 216, 234, 237, 243, 258
ensures 106
ensuring 12, 113, 229, 248-249
entail 51
entering 250
Enterprise 222, 251
entire 156, 178
entities 48
entity 3
equally 263
equipment 20, 23, 229, 235, 251
equipped 38
equitably 32, 237
errors 108, 157, 238
escalated 220
essential 86, 237
essentials 117, 218
establish 77, 97, 184, 205
estimate 49, 52, 54, 140-141, 173, 175, 182, 202, 255
estimated 35, 38, 52, 59, 183-184, 202, 252-253
estimates 6, 35, 48, 72, 138, 141, 143, 152, 173, 181, 185, 198, 247
Estimating 6, 159, 175, 183-184
estimation 138-139
etcetera 49, 118
ethical 120, 254
ethics 205
ethnic 109
Evaluate 88, 136, 157, 180, 194
evaluated 88, 214, 230
evaluating 89
evaluation 64, 77, 81, 95, 237, 258-259
evaluative 220
evaluators 240

events 26, 78, 83, 88, 174, 207
everyday 1, 70
everyone 32, 43, 189
everything 47, 227
evidence 13, 203-204, 214, 222, 250, 258
evolution 46
evolve 97
exactly 196, 230
examined 41
Example 4, 11, 15, 20, 99, 153
examples 10-11, 139
exceed 154, 167
exceeded 258
exceeding 55, 196
excellence 10, 32
excellent 58
excelling 196
except 157
excited 1
exciting 237
exclude 79
execute 219, 242, 254, 256
executed 225
Executing 7, 152, 199, 219
execution 97, 132, 219, 233
executive 10, 123, 212
executives 116
Exercise 28, 167
exerted 262
existing 12, 99, 144, 151, 246
exists 145, 168
expanded 250
expect 114, 140, 176, 181, 263
expected 19, 34, 85, 116, 125, 173, 227, 243
expend 57
experience 37, 106, 112, 116, 205, 214, 252
expert 173
expertise 85, 141, 234
experts 32
expiration 168
explained 12
explicitly 113
explore 70, 206

exposures 89
expressed 131
extend 239
extensive 2
extent 13, 20-22, 45, 90, 138-139, 156, 250
external 1-2, 42, 110, 205, 208
facilitate 13, 20, 64, 98, 244
facing 18, 111
fact-based 244
factors 49, 79, 120, 134, 184
failed 49
failure 120, 126, 229
fairly 32
familiar 11
fashion 3, 31
favorable 246
feasible 54, 73, 128, 184, 201
feature 12
features 254
feedback 34, 43, 49, 195
feeling 1
fidelity 250
finalize 211, 213
finalized 15
finally 145
financial 52, 63, 69, 72, 107-108, 137, 139, 174, 204
finding 173
fingertips 12
finish 161, 165-166, 248
fiscal 264
flexible 56
focused 56
follow 101, 107, 111, 139, 167
followed 39, 142, 211, 224, 264
following 11, 13
for--and 103
forces 189
forecast 248
forecasts 157
forever 110
forget 12
formal 8, 122, 212, 244-245, 254, 259, 264
formally 36, 132, 157, 197

format 12, 151, 160
formats   238
formed 37
formula   14, 105
Formulate   30
formulated   140, 234
forward   2, 112, 115
forwarded   158, 194
foster   127, 203
frames 258
framework   127, 191
freaky   124
frequency   39, 96, 121
frequent   198, 211
frequently   50-51, 235
friend   111, 120, 123
friends 2
frontiers   91
fulfill   119
full-blown   53
full-scale   91
fulltime 197
function   143, 254, 259
functional   141, 193
functions   67, 105, 110, 147, 171, 196, 233
funded 256
funding   112, 123, 143, 152, 256
further   11
future   10, 55, 100-101, 117, 204, 239
gained 2, 67, 96, 98, 239
gather 13, 31, 34, 36-37, 40, 42, 46, 67, 69-70, 187
gathered   31, 63, 65, 67, 69-71, 76
gathering   33-35, 174, 216
general   84, 153, 229, 238, 242, 255
generally   221
generate   73, 75
generated   62, 247
generation   11, 74, 264
generic   2
geographic   137, 234
getting 2, 57, 185
global   87
govern 119

governance 26, 187, 195
governing 241
Government 156
graded 224
graphics 19
graphs 11
greatest 82
ground 63
grounds 251
grouped 164
groups 115, 136, 152, 159, 179, 187, 211, 215, 221
growth 65, 119
guarantee 90
guaranteed 34
guiding 230
handle 169, 235
handled 187
happen 22, 127, 165, 204, 209, 250
happening 209, 250
happens 10, 41, 49, 51, 117, 119, 123, 147, 183, 189, 260
hardest 52
hardly 248
hardware 153, 206
Havent 128, 201
Having 203
hazards 210
health 128, 230
hearing 109
helpdesk 223
helping 10, 143, 219
hidden 56
higher 157, 216
highest 21
high-level 31, 38, 146
highlight 2, 195, 203
Highly 69
high-tech 125
hijacking 115
hiring 98
historical 173, 183, 259
history 161
hitters 72
hitting 249

holders 131
holiday 2
honest 120
Honestly   2
horizon 126
housed   145
humans   10
hypotheses   61
identified   3, 25, 28, 41-42, 62, 64, 72, 85, 88, 132, 138-139, 152, 164, 179, 193, 195, 198, 215, 217, 230
identify 1, 12-13, 19-21, 62, 66, 89, 133, 174, 183, 193, 246
identity 236
ignore 27
ignoring   116
images 146
imbedded   96
impact 7, 37, 48-49, 54-55, 57-59, 84, 126, 185, 194, 203-207, 219, 225, 232, 240, 256, 264
impacted   54, 151, 262
impacts   47, 57, 175, 204, 263
implement   18, 58, 75, 93, 242
implicit 121
importance   216, 237
important   26-27, 63, 66, 74, 105, 108, 111, 119, 123-124, 131, 142, 171, 174, 186, 189, 199, 213, 235, 237
improve   4, 12, 74, 77, 79-83, 85-87, 91, 133, 171, 181, 189, 233, 242, 256-257, 262
improved   2, 79, 83, 90-91, 95, 256
improving   80, 222
inadequate   1
incentives   98
incident   204, 228
include   20, 79, 85, 150, 161, 213-214, 223, 229, 237
included   4, 10, 22, 47, 176, 183, 189, 201, 223, 252-253, 260
INCLUDES   12
including   28, 30, 43-44, 52, 59, 74, 95, 101-102, 133, 216, 239, 247, 258, 263
increase   90, 120, 188, 207, 246
increased   108
increasing   109, 228
incurring   157
in-depth   11, 13
indicate   66, 102, 125

indicated 94, 258
indicators 28, 47, 56, 61, 63, 71, 73, 83, 102, 202, 230
indirect 51, 156-157, 181
indirectly 3
individual 54, 132, 138, 161, 234, 245, 252, 259, 262
industry 1-2, 102, 120, 126, 231
influence 91, 123, 131, 135, 199, 228, 262
inform 237
informal 244
informed 115, 193
ingrained 99
inherent 123
in-house 2, 133
initial 37, 114, 134, 177, 259
initially 43
initiated 136, 183, 226
Initiating 4, 118, 131
initiative 13, 191
Innovate 77
innovation 58, 64, 74, 86, 95, 116, 127, 258
innovative 118, 183
in-process 61
inputs 37, 58, 67, 98
inservice 259
inside 23
insight 68, 73
insights 1-2, 11
inspection 204
Instead 2
insure 115
integrate 82, 100, 114
integrity 21, 111, 225
intended 3, 82, 204, 242
INTENT 18, 30, 46, 61, 77, 93, 105
intention 3
intentions 230
interact 110
interest 110, 136, 209, 215, 221, 240
interested 136
interests 28
interface 179, 206
intergroup 236
internal 1, 3, 42, 65, 110, 117, 157-158, 194, 204

interpret 13
intervals 212
interview 1, 127
introduce 201
introduced 151, 236, 242
inventory 181
invest 70
investing 2
investment 21, 47, 66, 191
investor 53
invoice 232
invoices 197
involve 115, 136
involved 22, 27, 36, 53, 67, 70, 73, 89, 109, 137, 146, 150, 152, 174, 187, 194, 196, 205, 211, 215, 219, 221, 243, 261, 263
involves 95
involving 229
issues 20, 24-25, 27-28, 132, 146, 150-151, 169, 180, 188, 204, 220, 233
itself 3, 23, 159
judgment 173
justified 100
justify 204
killer 118
knowing 258
knowledge 1-2, 12, 37, 42-43, 67, 83, 85, 96, 98-99, 104, 112, 121-122, 185, 217, 229, 235, 239, 260
labeled 194
labeling 230
lacked 102
lacking 264
largely 63
larger 56
latest 11
leader 19, 68, 75, 83
leaders 37, 43, 75, 96, 118
leadership 28, 32, 35, 86, 118, 128
learned 1, 9, 98, 120, 191, 254, 262-265
learning 95, 99, 104
lesson 262-263
lessons 9, 91, 98, 120, 191, 254, 262, 264-265
Leveling 164
levels 21, 28, 35, 63, 73, 83, 101-102, 128, 188, 246, 258

leverage 34, 87, 98, 106, 183
leveraged 42
liability 3
licensed 3
lifecycle 49
lifecycles 85
Lifetime 12
likelihood 77, 82, 204, 209
likely 86, 123, 186, 207, 227
limitation 48
limited 12, 156
Linked 38, 227
listed 178
listen 111, 126
little 2
locally 80, 197
located 197
location 217, 228
logged 224
logical 156, 169, 247
logically 160
longer 1
long-term 96, 113, 122
looked 1
looking 20, 182
losing 49
losses 24, 40
lowest 168
magnitude 83
maintain 93, 111, 119
maintained 91, 157, 245
makers 89, 99, 131-132
making 19, 64, 79, 91, 118, 191-192, 219, 239
manage 36-37, 39, 48, 56, 74-75, 79, 81-82, 84-85, 121, 133, 140, 142, 148, 151, 177, 180-181, 191, 200, 205, 236, 246, 251
manageable 39, 91, 173
managed 10, 62-63, 66, 80, 83-84, 91, 98, 100, 224, 254
management 5-7, 11-12, 21-22, 26, 30, 37, 44, 58, 67-68, 70-71, 73, 75, 78, 80-83, 88, 90, 105-106, 117, 121, 132, 138-140, 142-144, 150-151, 156-157, 159-160, 171, 173-174, 176-182, 185, 187, 191, 197-201, 205, 207-208, 211-212, 215, 217-219, 222-223, 228-229, 233, 235, 239, 243, 248, 250-251, 254, 256, 259, 261, 263

manager   10, 12, 23, 35, 40, 122, 151, 174, 208, 211, 213, 215, 221, 254
Managers   4, 130, 174
manages   80, 89, 140, 253
managing   4, 81, 130, 135
mandatory   225
manner   24, 132, 223-224, 247, 254
mantle 106
Mapping   62, 70, 73
market 19, 133, 248, 258
marketer   10
Marketing   110
markets   23
master 156
material   133, 165, 258
materials   3, 235
matrices   148
Matrix 4-7, 136, 148, 193, 207
matter 32, 47, 56, 236
maximize   239
maximizing   117
maximum   131
meaning   163
meaningful   57, 106, 157
measurable   40-41, 220, 244
measure   4, 12, 20, 22, 34, 42, 46, 48-49, 51, 54, 58-59, 71, 74, 77, 79, 83, 89, 91, 94, 97, 99, 103, 159, 183, 190
measured   48, 50-51, 54, 56-57, 84, 98, 103, 189, 237
measures   47, 50-53, 56-57, 61, 63, 67, 73-74, 83, 102, 138, 188, 209, 219, 224
measuring   93, 229
mechanical   3
mechanism   223, 263
mechanisms   192
medium   236, 248
meeting   33, 44, 103, 185, 198, 211, 216, 221, 235
meetings   34-35, 44-45, 131, 150, 211, 235
megatrends   119
member   7-8, 32, 114, 124, 128, 172, 199, 221, 238
members   1, 30-32, 34, 41, 43, 69, 98, 139, 150, 197, 199, 201, 212-213, 223, 233-235, 237-238, 241, 244-245
membership   238
memorable   189

message 98, 218
messages 199, 234
method 138, 175, 190, 236-237
methods 34, 39, 54, 70, 184, 213, 217, 234
metrics 6, 35, 68, 98, 180, 189
milestone 5, 165, 168, 179
milestones 44, 135, 157, 167, 259
minimal 236
minimize 206, 219, 256
minimizing 117
minimum 252
minority 28
minutes 33, 84, 211
missed 53, 109
missing 64, 127, 163-164
mission 68, 73, 124, 230
mitigate 86, 204, 256
mitigated 2, 202
mitigation 140, 179, 201
mobile 238
modeling 63
models 19, 47, 68, 152
modified 97
modifier 189
module 144
moment 107
moments 75
momentum 109, 114
Monday 1
monetary 22
monitor 94, 96, 101-103, 142, 183, 197
monitored 93, 100, 175
monitoring 8, 93-95, 100, 104, 151, 169, 178, 216, 224, 230, 242
monthly 246
months 1, 84, 88
morning 1
motivate 110, 244
motivated 132, 198
motivation 24, 94, 134
motive 191
moving 115
narrative 165

narrow 64
national 139
nature 157, 246
nearest 14
nearly 110
necessary 67-68, 75-76, 107, 118, 183, 193, 213, 220, 226, 232, 236
needed 2, 18, 20, 22, 25-26, 37, 67-69, 94, 97, 104, 131, 133, 146, 153, 175, 200, 215, 238, 240, 264
negative 106
negatively 220, 262
negotiate 121
negotiated 127, 217
neither 3
network 5, 167, 178, 244-245
Neutral 13, 18, 30, 46, 61, 77, 93, 105
normal 99, 157
notice 3, 138, 173
noticing 228
notified 199, 202, 260
noting 224
number 29, 45, 57, 60, 76, 92, 104, 129, 163, 251, 266
numbers 123
numerous 260
objection 21
objective 10, 50, 133, 207, 227
objectives 2, 25-27, 30, 38, 68, 73, 95, 101, 108, 116, 125, 131, 138, 159, 177, 198, 200, 203-204, 209, 221, 244, 262
observe 196
observed 91
obsolete 119
obstacles 19, 183
obtain 111, 263
obtained 43, 132
obtaining 58
obviously 13
occurrence 202
occurring 87
occurs 23, 53, 94, 219
offerings 74, 89
office 197, 222, 260
Officer 1
officials 261

onboarding 212
one-time 10
ongoing 88, 98, 175
on-going 142-143, 197
opened 247
operate 234
operates 126
operating 8, 51-52, 94, 157, 234
operation 103, 185
operations 12, 93, 98-100, 185
operators 101
opinion 216
opinions 206
opponent 227
opposed 199
opposite 122, 126
opposition 109
optimal 81, 252
optimize 91, 93
optimized 106
option 108
options 23, 182, 239
ordered 1
organized 163
orient 103
oriented 143
original 177, 212, 227
originally 143
originate 99
others 131, 174, 184, 193, 199-200, 202, 206-207, 223, 245, 262
otherwise 3, 239
outcome 13, 90, 232
outcomes 79, 93, 115, 183, 204, 249, 256, 264
outlined 95
output 34, 62-64, 69, 71-75, 96, 102, 150
outputs 37, 66-68, 71-72, 98, 169, 174
outside 90, 131, 133, 235
outsource 64, 174, 219, 260
outweigh 50
overall 12-13, 27, 47, 100, 125, 128, 131, 167, 188, 228, 252, 264
overcome 183
overhead 157, 246
overheads 142

overlook 240
overlooked 219
overruns 193
oversight 65, 180, 197, 239
overtime 169
owners 154
ownership 33, 96
packages 157, 194
packaging 230
paradigms 126
paragraph 124
parallel 168
parameters 94
paramount 201
Pareto 72
parking 235
Parties 2, 89, 261
partners 27, 36, 89, 97, 110, 118, 120, 263
patterns 86
paycheck 128
paying 110
payment 197, 258, 260
payments 180
pending 225
people 10, 28, 58-59, 65, 69, 83, 89, 103, 106, 110, 113, 117-119, 121-122, 126, 136, 152, 159, 187, 190-191, 193-194, 203, 205, 207, 209, 219, 222, 234, 242, 248, 256
perceive 127
percent 124
percentage 148
perception 92, 120
perform 28, 31-32, 144, 161, 171, 174, 209, 254
performed 88, 148, 161-162, 232, 247
perhaps 26, 248
period 81
periodic 143
permission 3
person 3, 20, 199
personal 123
personally 148
personnel 21-22, 70, 93, 167, 178-179, 191, 230, 258-259
pertaining 132
pertinent 93

phases 49, 88, 138, 145, 199, 242, 256
pieces 215
pitfalls 123
planet 103
planned 95, 98-100, 143, 145, 156, 162, 175, 204, 256, 262
planners 99
planning 4, 11, 94, 98, 138, 140, 150, 152, 157, 169, 219, 222, 229, 243
platform 238
players 90
playing 2
pocket 183
pockets 183
points 29, 45, 60, 71, 76, 92, 104, 128, 165, 191
policies 251
policing 250
policy 30, 83, 99, 169, 187, 204, 259
political 39, 110, 138
portfolio 124
portion 2
portray 72
position 136, 196
positioned 184
positions 136
positive 88, 106, 109, 229, 236
positively 262
possible 49, 56, 64, 75, 78, 93, 108, 180, 198, 229, 236
potential 21, 49, 66, 85, 87-88, 119, 125, 150, 193, 209, 242, 246
practical 73, 77-78, 93, 222
practice 197
practices 12, 86, 98, 139-140, 238, 254, 265
precaution 3
predicting 93
prediction 163
preferred 263
pre-filled 11
prepare 264
prepared 1, 182
preparing 236, 262
present 101, 117, 123, 145, 173, 197-198, 217, 236
presented 1, 24
preserve 44

preserved 68
pressing 132
prevent 51, 185, 204, 238
preventive 209
prevents 19
previous 42, 132, 178, 252
previously 136, 225
priced 157
primary 55, 134
priorities 52-53, 55, 58
priority 53, 57, 164
probable 208
probably 171
problem 18, 20, 22-24, 26, 28, 30, 40, 42, 44-45, 47, 67, 73, 137, 222, 227, 244, 248
problems 18, 20, 23, 25-26, 28, 82, 87, 94, 115, 138, 151
procedure 187, 259
procedures 12, 81, 94, 101-102, 142, 157, 169, 173, 178, 192, 198, 212, 216, 224, 228-229, 235, 246, 259
proceed 206, 246
proceeding 177, 212
process 4, 6-8, 10, 12, 31, 34, 37-39, 54, 62-70, 72-76, 79, 91, 95-96, 98-103, 131-132, 138-139, 142, 144, 146, 148, 150, 152-153, 159, 169, 174-175, 178, 187, 191-192, 197, 201, 207-208, 212, 214, 219, 223, 227, 229, 232-233, 239, 242, 248-250, 253, 256, 259, 263
processes 1, 47, 57, 61, 64-65, 67-68, 70-71, 74-75, 95, 98-99, 136, 139, 153, 180, 206, 211, 217-218, 225, 230, 235, 238, 242, 254
produce 1, 72, 133, 169, 221, 232, 242
produced 69, 88
producing 148, 150
product 3, 52, 63, 74, 116, 118, 143, 145, 150-151, 185, 188, 207, 221-222, 226, 233, 248-249, 251, 262-264
production 40, 88, 108, 136, 235
products 3, 20, 24, 58, 106, 114, 133-134, 148, 157, 182, 206, 220-221, 225
profession 202
profile 204, 229
program 23, 51, 73, 101, 133, 188, 204, 242-243, 259
programs 222-223, 230
progress 33, 54, 101, 111, 118, 157, 183, 191-192, 216, 219-220
prohibited 157

project 4-6, 8, 10-11, 18, 21, 28, 39, 53, 62, 67, 81, 95, 99-100, 105, 110, 112, 115, 119, 122, 125-126, 130-140, 142-144, 148, 150-154, 159-161, 163, 165, 167-168, 171-183, 185-188, 195, 197-201, 203-208, 211-213, 215-216, 218-226, 232-233, 240, 242, 244-245, 247-248, 252, 254-258, 261-265
projected 193
projection 206
projects 4, 58, 124, 130-131, 139, 142, 148, 174, 177, 181-182, 185, 201, 221-222, 248-249, 251, 265
promising 118
promote 58, 65, 137, 173
promptly 220, 237
proofing 91
proper 102
properly 41, 43, 258-259
proposal 145, 165, 213-214
proposals 99, 214
proposed 18, 49, 59, 252
protect 62, 122
protected 68, 235
protection 117
protocols 187, 234
proved 254
provide 23, 68, 115, 125, 135, 140, 144, 147, 156-157, 168, 183, 194, 197, 237, 244
provided 2, 14, 95, 137, 142-143, 179, 214, 230, 235
providers 89
providing 102, 135, 165
provision 228
published 259
publisher 3
pulled 124
purchase 10, 232
purchasing 1-2
purpose 4, 12, 124, 131, 133, 150, 184, 191, 236-237
pursuing 2
pushing 124
qualified 32, 66, 69, 72, 151, 159, 174
qualifies 67, 76
qualify 57, 65-66
qualities 20
quality 6-7, 12, 46, 56, 62, 72, 74, 82, 94, 102, 123, 139, 142-143, 151, 178-179, 187, 189-192, 196-197, 211, 220, 228-230, 233, 259

quantified 101
quantify 57
question 13, 18, 30, 46, 61, 77, 93, 105, 107, 191
questions 10-11, 13, 73, 220
quickly 12, 68, 75
radically 68
raised 151
raising 139
raters 238
rather 115
rating 213, 224, 238
rational 247
rationale 215, 227
reached 26
reaching 116
reaction 206
readiness 40, 142, 217
readings 103
realistic 26, 120, 131, 140, 173, 177, 237
Reality 205, 236
realize 2, 48
realized 124, 255
realizing 1
really 10, 25, 41, 193
reason 122
reasonable 91, 117, 141, 143, 198
reasons 32, 189
re-assign 164
reassigned 185
rebuild 118
recast 182
receive 11-12, 35, 57, 199
received 33, 125, 237, 264
recently 123
receptive 258
recipient 20, 260
recognised 86
recognize 4, 18, 21-23, 25-26, 56, 86, 90
recognized 20-21, 24, 26-28, 65, 200, 229, 236, 240, 259
recognizes 23
recommend 111, 123
record 192
recorded 259

recording 3, 224
records 67, 126, 157, 215, 260
recovery 57, 152
recurrence 209
redefine 26, 33
re-design 76
reduce 50, 58, 138, 156, 187, 204, 228, 237
reducing 103, 109
referenced 189
references 266
reflect 67, 96, 101, 104, 153, 157, 262
reflected 245
reform 99, 114, 128
reforms 18, 49, 54
refreshed 2
regarding 116, 123, 213-214, 222
Register 4, 7, 135, 199, 203
regular 33, 35, 65, 179, 251-252
regularly 34, 43, 131, 185, 251
regulatory 20, 233
reinforce 173
reject 144
rejecting 144
rejection 229
relate 71, 225
related 19, 59, 64, 99, 151, 188, 196, 199, 248
relating 185
relation 19, 23, 78, 124
relations 110, 203
relative 101, 213, 237
relatively 122
release 199
released 258
releases 253
relevant 40, 48, 68, 126, 205, 233
reliable 38, 209
relieved 2
remain 43
remaining 178, 183, 262
remember 175
remove 209
remunerate 85
repair 180, 198

repeat 132
repeatable   207
rephrased   12
replace   56
replacing   144
replicated   263
report 7-8, 80, 103, 204, 221, 233, 244, 252, 262, 264
reported   189, 215, 249
reporting   71, 97, 128, 156, 179, 224
reports 2, 57, 104, 135, 158, 179, 194
repository   142
represent   84, 225-226
reproduced   3
reputation   108
request   7, 73, 213, 223, 225-226
requested   3, 79, 132, 226
requests   207, 223-224, 259
require 45, 53, 71, 97, 99, 169, 215, 244, 265
required   20, 32, 35, 37, 40, 43, 58, 70-71, 81, 83, 92, 102, 132, 156, 161-164, 175, 182, 191, 200-201, 205, 217, 234, 259, 262-263
requiring   135, 260
research   19, 116, 118, 230, 235
reserved   3
reserves   157
reside 85
resistance   217
resolution   68, 83, 150
resolve 20, 24, 28, 164, 235
resolved   220
resource   5-6, 131, 139, 143, 145, 152, 157, 159, 164, 169, 171, 197-198, 222
resources   2, 4, 10, 21-22, 25, 27, 38, 42, 50, 73, 83, 97, 100, 102, 109, 113, 140, 142-143, 145, 159, 162-164, 167, 171, 174, 178, 181, 183, 185, 216-217, 235-236, 251
respect   3
respected   259
respond   138, 193, 203
responded   14
response   19, 23, 94-97, 102, 201, 252, 264
responses   79, 106, 203, 230
responsive   183
restrict 147

result   72, 84, 88, 151, 183, 185, 189, 226, 245, 260, 262-263
resultant   214
resulted   97
resulting   63
results   11, 34, 43, 56, 74, 77-80, 82-83, 85, 89-90, 95, 102, 131, 163, 177, 179, 182, 184, 188, 191, 219, 230, 243, 250
Retain 105
retained   69
retaining   173
retention   48
retrospect   124
return   88, 107, 191
revenue   25, 50
revenues   55
review 12, 40, 70, 141, 178, 186, 204, 227, 231, 235, 259
reviewed   38, 189, 212, 230
reviewers   237
reviews 167, 179, 205
revised 72, 97
revisions   214, 260
revisit   228
reward 54, 58, 75, 173, 222
rewarded   21
rewards   98
rework 50, 55
rights   3
roll-out 217
routine 100, 246
safeguards   238
safety   106, 251
sampling   187
satisfied   127, 144, 262
satisfies 248
savings 35, 48, 51, 72
scalable   89
scenario   38, 40, 173
scenes 2
schedule   5-6, 35, 53, 128, 143-144, 156, 159-160, 167-168, 177-179, 194, 203, 212, 223, 226, 233, 246, 253
scheduled   131, 157, 180, 198
schedules   151, 156, 167
scheduling   157
scheme   95

Science 62, 175
scientific 175
Scorecard 4, 14-16
scorecards 98
Scores 16
scoring 12
Screen 223
seamless 115
second 14
secret 2
secrets 1
section 14, 29, 45, 60, 76, 92, 104, 128-129
sector 248
securing 55, 119
security 22, 61, 78, 96, 101, 135, 153, 207, 225
segmented 42
segments 33, 115
select 64, 100
selected 84, 140, 183, 246
selecting 72, 108, 216, 219
Selection 7, 213
self-help 2
sellers 3
selling 112, 165
senior 96, 105, 118, 128
sensitive 55, 138
sequence 156, 161
sequenced 160
sequencing 128, 211
series 13
service 1-4, 10, 52, 89, 92, 102, 118, 151, 185, 188, 204, 221-222, 259, 264
services 3, 45, 54, 58, 60, 107, 114, 229-230, 235, 242, 252-253, 255, 258, 260
serving 230
session 157
setbacks 68, 75
setting 120, 122
several 69
severely 76
shared 98, 139, 147, 184, 228
sharing 83, 99, 217
sheets 145

shifts 25
shopping 1
shortly 258
short-term 236
should 10, 24-26, 28, 31, 34, 40, 52, 57, 59, 62-65, 69-70, 79-80, 85, 90, 99, 103, 112, 120-122, 126-127, 135, 139, 144, 161, 163, 171, 174-175, 178, 181, 185, 187, 189, 193, 195-196, 202-204, 206-209, 213-214, 217, 219, 223, 225, 238-239, 242, 256, 262
signature 113
signatures 169
signed 151
signers 261
similar 39, 42, 72, 74, 89, 161, 163
simple 122, 244, 248
simply 11, 228
single 124, 156
single-use 10
situation 2, 27, 46, 177, 243, 248
situations 103
skeptical 110
skills 23, 28, 65, 111, 122, 174, 194, 202-203, 207, 217, 229, 236, 239, 245, 250
smallest 88
smooth 265
smoothly 218
soccer 1
social 110, 236
societal 119
software 20, 144, 173, 201-202, 205-206, 220, 253
solicit 34
solution 1, 58, 68, 73, 77-78, 81-84, 87, 89, 91, 93, 252
solutions 53, 78, 81, 87-88, 100, 206
solved 24
solving 244
Someone 10
something 110, 185, 187, 207
Sometimes 53
source 7, 112, 114, 209, 213
sources 34, 70, 72
special 43, 95, 134
specific 11, 23, 30, 40-41, 66, 107, 163, 168-169, 171, 196, 215, 221, 225, 257
specified 116, 156, 159, 258, 263

specify 229
Speech   146
spending   2
spoken 123
sponsor   26, 133, 179, 215, 217, 220
sponsors   27, 131
spread 94, 98
stable 205
staffed 42
staffing 28, 98, 140, 152, 197
stages 140, 259
standard   10, 102-103, 169, 197, 252-253
standards   12-13, 94, 99, 101, 104, 189, 198, 225, 238, 250, 259
standing   258
started 11, 167
starting 12, 139
start-up   136
stated 108, 113, 156, 188, 190, 256
statement   5, 13, 82, 142, 150, 153, 160, 181
statements   14, 29, 40, 44-45, 60, 67, 76, 92, 104, 129, 191, 230
statistics   151
Status 7-8, 65, 212, 221, 233, 248, 252
statutory   233
steady 46
steering   180, 197, 212
stopper   146
storage   192, 245
stored 145
stories 31
strategic   53, 101, 108, 159, 204, 251
strategies   109, 114, 138, 150, 152, 179, 201, 227-228, 250, 264
strategy   27, 35, 50, 55, 78, 85, 87, 102, 106, 109, 125, 128, 152, 160, 182, 199, 204, 211, 228, 258, 262
Stream 62, 70
strength   136
strengths   180, 254
stretch 122
strict   67
strive   122
Strongly   13, 18, 30, 46, 61, 77, 93, 105
structural   236

structure   5-6, 58, 81, 122, 133, 154, 171, 208, 245
Structured   123
structures   244
stubborn   121
stupid 120
subdivided   194
subfactor   214
subject 11-12, 32
Subjective   190
subjects   69
submitted   225
sub-teams   236
succeed   58, 110
success   20-21, 31-32, 36, 42, 51, 58, 77, 83, 85, 103, 105, 107, 115, 118, 120, 125-126, 131, 134, 142, 181, 221, 228, 237-238
successes   113
successful   1, 65, 103, 116, 119, 125, 138-139, 171, 186, 219, 222, 263
succession   97
suffered   237
sufficient   138, 242, 259
suggest   223, 229
suggested   94, 225-226
suitable   201
summary   158, 194
Sunday   1
superior   1
supervisor   234
supplier   80, 110, 179, 258
suppliers   37, 63-64, 118, 216
supplies   255
supply 46
support   3, 10, 27, 64, 97-98, 103, 105, 109, 137, 143, 147, 169, 217-218, 229, 234, 252
supported   72, 139, 250
supporters   137
supporting   92, 102, 192, 212
supports   234
surface   94, 264
SUSTAIN   4, 91, 105
sustained   182
sustaining   96, 234
symptom   18, 51

system 12, 33, 72-73, 95, 106, 118, 144, 146-147, 153, 156-157, 194, 225, 229-230, 238, 242, 248-249
systems 1, 71, 74-75, 85, 87, 98, 136, 142, 173, 179, 213, 229, 248, 255
tables 188
tackle 51
tactics 227-228
tailored 2, 213
takers 150
taking 50, 222
talent 66, 128
talking 10
tangible 250
target 44, 128, 179
targets 122, 220, 249
tasked 96
technical 85, 131, 141, 147, 157, 213
techniques 68, 132, 140, 174
technology 1, 56, 84, 102, 118, 134, 136, 146, 174, 201, 230, 234-235
template 178
templates 10-11
tender 258
testable 36
tested 19
testing 188, 201, 250
thematic 137
themselves 1, 119, 245
theory 94
thcrefore 258
therein 247
things 88, 181, 189, 201, 206, 211, 242
thinking 62, 90, 116
third- 89
thorough 90, 225
thought 234
threat 23, 111, 237
threaten 177
threats 1-2, 185
through 65, 72, 118, 150, 223, 228, 250
throughout 3, 117, 167
Thursday 1
tighter 110

time-based 246
time-bound 40
timeframe 70, 183
timeframes 20
timeline 226
timely 24, 31, 132, 205, 223-224, 233, 235
timetable 167, 259
Timing 199
together 118
tolerances 85, 240
tolerated 161
tomorrow 103, 128, 132
toolkit 1-2
toolkits 1-2
topics 85
touched 146
toward 103, 222
towards 2, 68
tracked 150, 198, 223
tracking 40, 100, 151-152
traction 111
trade-in 259
trademark 3
trademarks 3
trained 41, 43, 187, 201, 213
training 18, 25, 28, 63, 70, 95, 98, 102, 185, 217, 221, 230, 235, 238-239, 259, 264
trainings 22
Transfer 14, 29, 45, 60, 76, 92, 96, 98, 104, 129, 185, 208, 252
transition 128
translated 41
travel 235
trends 63, 66, 73, 83, 127, 151, 188, 207
trigger 85, 92
triggers 82, 186, 211
trophy 106
trouble 110
trying 10, 110, 115, 188-189, 209
typical 131, 240
ultimate 112
unaware 1
unclear 37

uncovered 2
underlying 86
undermine 110
underruns 193
understand 30, 75, 131, 174, 250
understood 87, 91, 125, 202, 245
undertake 70, 204
undertaken 259
underway 79
uninformed 115
unique 2, 113, 165, 181, 234
Unless 10
unplanned 235
unprepared 1
unpriced 247
unproven 206
unresolved 169, 179
update 1, 185
updated 11-12, 67, 143, 167, 173, 198, 211
updates 12, 98, 252
upfront 218, 243
upload 235
up-sell 107
usability 77
useful 86, 94, 152, 154, 182, 264
usefully 12
usually 1
utilised 216
utility 175
utilized 173, 265
utilizing 1, 84
validate 57, 249
validated 31, 38, 62, 74
Validation 249
Validity 147
valuable 10
values 96, 118, 230, 259
variables 75, 96, 227
variance 8, 156, 194, 236-237, 246-247
-variance 181
variances 142, 156, 215, 246
variation 18, 34, 70, 72, 103
variety 83

vendor 80, 131, 168, 179, 197, 206
vendors 24, 72, 89, 142, 151, 180, 259
verified 12, 31, 38, 62, 165
verify 46-47, 50, 52-53, 55-60, 97, 101, 103, 151, 246, 248, 260
verifying 51, 53-54
version 253, 266
versions 34, 37
versus 145
vested 110, 209
viable 100, 154
viewpoint 262
viewpoints 262
violated 153
virtual 238
Vision 118, 230
visits 179
visualize 175
voices 135
volatile 87
volatility 202
volume 158
Volumes 136
vulnerable 136
waited 2
walking 2
warranty 3
weaknesses 136-137, 153, 214, 254
website 223
weeknights 1
Whence 250
whether 10, 95, 114, 133, 263
wholesaler 179
widespread 101
widgets 179
willing 205
wishes 229
within 1-2, 70, 81, 133, 163, 175, 215, 217, 222, 225, 234, 254, 258
without 1, 3, 14, 118-119, 139, 206, 226, 250, 260
worked 132, 182, 205, 265
workers 109
workflow 73, 227
workforce 28, 83, 115, 118, 198

working   2, 95, 98, 152, 195, 207, 227
Worksheet   6, 175, 183
worried   237
worst-case   40
writing 128, 148
written 3
yesterday   24
youhave   157
yourself   115, 120, 124

Made in the USA
Middletown, DE
25 June 2024